W9-CNH-643

Previous Books by Manz and Pearce

అ *Share, Don't Take the Lead,* Craig L. Pearce, Charles
C. Manz, and Henry P. Sims, Jr. Information Age
Publishing, 2014.

Previous Books by Manz

అ *Self-Leadership: The Definitive Guide to Personal
Excellence,* Christopher P. Neck, Charles C. Manz, and
Jeffery D. Houghton. Sage, 2017.

అ *Shared Entrepreneurship: A Path to Engaged Employee
Ownership,* Frank Shipper, S. B. Adams, M. O. Brown,
Charles C. Manz, O. P. Roche, M. D. Street, V. L. Street,
and C. H. Weer. Palgrave MacMillan, 2014.

అ *Mastering Self-Leadership: Empowering Yourself for
Personal Excellence,* Charles C. Manz. Prentice-Hall,
1992. Charles C. Manz and Christopher P. Neck, 2nd
Ed. 1999; Neck and Manz, 3rd Ed. 2003, 4th Ed. 2007,
5th Ed. 2010, 6th Ed. 2013. Translated into several
languages.

అ *Fit to Lead: The Proven 8-Week Solution for Shaping up
Your Body, Your Mind and Your Career,* Christpher Neck,
Theodore Mitchell, Charles C. Manz, T. Thompson, and
J. Tornelli-Mitchell. 1st Ed., St. Martins, 2004, 2nd Ed.,
Carpenter's Son Publishing, 2012. Also released on CD
and CD-ROM.

❧ *The Leadership Wisdom of Jesus,* Charles C. Manz. Berrett-Koehler, hardcover 1998, paperback, 1999, 2nd Ed. 2005, 3rd Ed. 2011. Translated into nine languages and audio version released.

❧ **Nice Guys Can Get the Corner Office: Eight Strategies for Winning in Business Without Being a Jerk,** R. Edleman, T. Hiltabiddle, and Charles C. Manz. Portfolio Books Penguin Publishers, 2008.

❧ *The Virtuous Organization: Insights from Some of the World's Leading Management Thinkers,* Charles C. Manz, K. Cameron, Karen P. Manz, and R. D. Marx (Eds.). World Scientific Publishers, 2008.

❧ *The Greatest Leader Who Wasn't: A Leadership Fable,* Charles C. Manz. Walk the Talk, 2005.

❧ *Temporary Sanity: Instant Self-Leadership Strategies for Turbulent Times,* Charles C. Manz. Financial Times Prentice-Hall, 2005.

❧ *The Power to Choose How You Feel: Keys to Creating and Maintaining a Positive Attitude* (short book format), Charles C. Manz. Successories, 2004.

❧ *Emotional Discipline: The Power to Choose How You Feel,* Charles C. Manz. Berrett-Koehler, 2003. Translated into seven foreign languages. Winner of Foreward Reviews Magazine Gold Award for best book of the year in the personal development (self-help) category.

- *The Power of Failure: 27 Ways to Turn Life's Setbacks into Success,* Charles C. Manz. Berrett-Koehler, 2002. Translated into twelve languages.

- *The New SuperLeadership: Leading Others to Lead Themselves,* Charles C. Manz and Henry P. Sims, Jr. Berrett-Koehler, 2001. Translated into Korean and Japanese.

- *The Wisdom of Solomon at Work: Ancient Virtues for Living and Leading Today,* Charles C. Manz, Karen Manz, Robert D. Marx, and Christopher Neck. Berrett-Koehler, 2001. Translated into five languages.

- *Team Work and Group Dynamics,* Greg Stewart, Charles C. Manz, and Henry P. Sims, Jr. Wiley, 1998. Translated into Spanish.

- *For Team Members Only: Making Your Workplace Team Productive and Hassle-Free,* Charles C. Manz, Christopher Neck, James Mancuso, and Karen Manz. AMACOM, 1997.

- *Company of Heroes: Unleashing the Power of Self-Leadership,* Henry P. Sims, Jr., and Charles C. Manz. Wiley, 1996. Translated into Korean.

- *Business Without Bosses: How Self-Managing Teams are Building High-Performing Companies,* Charles C. Manz and Henry P. Sims, Jr. Wiley, hardcover 1993, paperback, 1995. Translated into six languages, selection by Fortune Book Club, selection of Audio-Track audio abridgement.

- *Self-Leadership: A Skill Building Series,* Charles C. Manz. Organizational Design and Development, 1993.

- *SuperLeadership: Leading Others to Lead Themselves,* Charles C. Manz and Henry P. Sims, Jr. Prentice-Hall Press, 1989 (hardcover), Berkley Books, 1990 (paperback). Selection of Executive Book Club (subsidiary of Macmillan Publishers), Fast Track, 1990 (audio abridgement) over 50,000 units. Translated into Japanese (audio), Korean, and Spanish. Winner of the Stybel-Peabody literary prize.

- *The Art of Self-Leadership,* Charles C. Manz. Prentice-Hall Press, 1983. Translated into Indonesian.

Previous Books by Pearce

- *The Drucker Difference,* Craig L. Pearce, Joseph Maciarello, and Hideki Yamawaki (Eds.). McGraw-Hill, 2010. Translated into nine languages.

- *Shared Leadership: Reframing the Hows and Whys of Leadership,* Craig L. Pearce and Jay A. Conger (Eds.). Sage, 2003. Cited more than 1,000 times.

TWISTED
LEADERSHIP

TWISTED LEADERSHIP

How to Engage the Full Talents
of Everyone in Your Organization

❧

Charles C. Manz
Craig L. Pearce

MAVEN HOUSE

Published by Maven House Press, 4 Snead Ct., Palmyra, VA 22963
610.883.7988 • www.mavenhousepress.com.

Special discounts on bulk quantities of Maven House Press books
are available to corporations, professional associations, and other
organizations. For details contact the publisher.

For information about subsidiary rights (translation, audio, book club,
serial, etc.) contact rights@mavenhousepress.com.

While this publication is designed to provide accurate and authoritative
information in regard to the subject matter covered, it is sold with the
understanding that the publisher is not engaged in rendering legal,
accounting, or other professional service. If legal advice or other expert
assistance is required, the services of a competent professional person
should be sought. — From the Declaration of Principles jointly adopted
by a Committee of the American Bar Association and a Committee of
Publishers and Associations

Library of Congress Control Number: 2017904454

Hardcover ISBN: 978-1-938548-86-4
ePUB ISBN: 978-1-938548-87-1
ePDF ISBN: 978-1-938548-88-8
Kindle ISBN: 978-1-938548-89-5

Printed in the United States of America.

10 9 8 7 6 5 4 3 2 1

Contents

❧

W E BEGIN with an extreme understatement . . .

These are interesting times for leadership.
Indeed, multitudes around the globe have unprecedented concern about the apparent trend toward centralization and abuse of power by national and business leaders alike.

In fact, the combination of the words *twisted* and *leadership* may bring to mind images of narcissism and self-serving destructive motives and action on the part of so many power holders who happen to be assigned the role of "leader."

From the outset we want to make clear that this book assigns a very different meaning to the words *twisted leadership*. We use these words in the spirit of arguably the best of martial arts, conflict management, and opportunity-focused social interaction strategies that channel not only collaborative but opposing energy and resistance to accomplish common good. The following is a summary of what we *do* and *do not* mean by *twisted leadership:*

TWISTED LEADERSHIP

IS NOT

ॐ

Centralized, Top-Down, Abusive,
Self-Serving, Corruption-Prone,
Role-Based Leadership

IS

ॐ

Intertwined, Synergistic,
Empowering, Developmental,
High-Involving,
Process-Based Leadership

Part One

❧

The Leadership Disease and Its Cure

I'S TIME TO GET TWISTED. Leadership is a mess these days. The vast majority of prescriptions for leadership available today are based on alchemy, and they're voiced by so-called thought leaders and self-proclaimed gurus who have little grounding in the science of leadership. What these purported experts are peddling are poison pills, which create and sustain the leadership disease.

The leadership disease is the overfocus on centralized, top-down, hierarchical leadership, where one designated individual lords influence over lower-level subordinates. The media feeds the myth surrounding charismatic and heroic visionary leaders, who are often portrayed as single-handedly inspiring and directing their organizations to new heights. Such simplistic portrayals of leadership are promulgated by the media and loved by the consuming public. Sadly, however, this portrayal of leadership is dangerous – it fosters corruption, abuse of power, and the waste of human talent.

The purpose of this book is to provide the antidote: twisted leadership. Twisted leadership encompasses a four-fold approach to overcoming the leadership disease. It's a new, potent, comprehensive cure that effectively twists the disease right out of the system. Moreover, the leadership cure we prescribe can twist opportunities out of seeming obstacles – such as learning and succeeding through "failure" and unleashing innovative power from disagreements and conflicts (that foster breakthrough ideas) . . . like twisting the juice from lemons to make lemonade.

Most importantly, the curative approach we prescribe in this book combines (twists together) complementary parts that create astounding leadership synergies. Imagine a rope as a leadership metaphor. Twisted leadership consists of four practical, complementary leadership strands, what we call the four Ss of twisted leadership: self-leadership, SuperLeadership, shared leadership, and socially responsible leadership. Each strand supports and adds to the strength of the others. The four Ss form a new kind of leadership that is comprehensive, strong, sustainable, and well-suited for the dynamic and complex times we live in. Each of these leadership types (strands of twisted leadership) has become an increasing focus of scientific research, and together they offer a potent, comprehensive cure for the leadership disease.

Chapter 1

అ

What Is the Leadership Disease?

UR BUSINESS, political, and not-for-profit world is afflicted by a leadership disease. What is this disease? It's the overly simplistic description, formulaic portrayal, and myopic encouragement of a model of leadership that focuses on centralized, top-down, hierarchical leadership (see Figure 1). There are many leaders who are infected with the disease – leadership goes to their heads. They think that upon ascension to a leadership role they become anointed in some manner and are thus smarter than everyone else. They begin to think that their will is more important than everyone else's. We've all met them.

We witness the leadership disease in all walks of life. We've even experienced it in academia, the one place in our world where democratic principles, inclusiveness,

The Leadership Disease

Figure 1. Image representing the centralized, top-down, leadership as a role perspective that results in corruption, abuses of power, and the waste of human talent.

and openness are thought to be practiced with the utmost rigor. Not always. We knew a dean who would best be described as a megalomaniac. He treated faculty in an arbitrary manner, bestowing benefits to those who told him he was fabulous, with a blind eye toward any measure of performance when it came to handing out rewards. Treating faculty this way wasn't good, but it was nothing compared to how he treated staff. He was so abusive to staff that it was sickening. People tried to modify his behavior. All the faculty and staff were even deposed in a grievance suit against him, but his buddy, a higher-level administrator (who was also an extreme narcissist), glossed over all his abuse of power. Many faculty and staff (the most successful ones) chose to leave the school because of the dean. These types of petty dictators, sorely infected with the leadership disease, are everywhere. The question, though, is why?

These "leaders" are often charming . . . in the beginning. And they tend to deliver short-term results. Over time, however, people come to understand them for what they are, and these disease-ridden leaders ultimately move on, only to infect new organizations. But how do they keep getting new, high-level positions where they can lord their power over others? One contributing factor is that many subordinates are just glad to get rid of them, and they fail to inform people in the new, unsuspecting organization of the leader's true nature. Another factor is that employment laws often discourage people from providing prospective employers the truth about these tyrants.

Educators share some of the responsibility for the leadership disease. Let's review some of the ideas behind the way leadership is typically viewed and taught today. For the most part, leadership definitions focus on downward influence exerted by someone occupying the role of a designated leader. These definitions assume an unequal distribution of power, where the person in the designated leadership role exerts power over those subordinates or followers below him or her. Perhaps the most egregious school of thought regarding leadership is based on agency theory, a theory that's extremely popular with business school professors. The essence of the theory is that most people are shirkers, and the principals of the organization have to guard against these shirkers engaging in "moral hazard" – irresponsible or self-serving decision making – and debilitating the organization. With these assumptions in mind, proponents of this theory advocate for extreme controls, as well as tightly bound rewards and sanctions, as the primary tools for keeping people in line. Is it any wonder that this type of thinking promotes power-hungry organizational dictators?

This perspective forms the foundation of much leadership thought and education, which promotes a myopic focus on a centralized and hierarchical approach to organizing and leading people. While enlightened consumers of leadership research would claim that views of leadership have progressed beyond the old image of top-down, autocratic bosses, leadership is still generally taught from the perspective of leadership-as-a-role – that someone has the role of leader, and others are followers. Leaders are taught to exert their authority to influence subordinates to comply with their desires.

This perspective on leadership became firmly embedded in management thinking during the turn of the 20th century, as part of the scientific management movement. Those who use this type of leadership are called strongman leaders or directive leaders. They employ a command and control style of leadership that uses fear and intimidation to obtain compliance.

An alternative type of leadership, transactional leadership, focuses on a more palatable influence that's based on rewards. But it still emphasizes top-down influence. And even the often more positively viewed transformational, visionary, and charismatic types of leadership, in which leaders rely on tools such as inspirational communication or a unifying vision of purpose, place the spotlight on the leader as the primary source of knowledge, decisions, and wisdom, in order to keep the shirkers in line.

The reality of the science of leadership is that some of these more touted leadership perspectives have come under question by an increasing number of leadership experts, challenging the romanticized notion of formal, top-down leaders. Unfortunately, these distorted perspectives remain significant influences on contemporary organizational thinking and practice. Why?

Social scientists point out that people, whether they know it or not, possess clear beliefs about how those in leadership roles should behave, and they judge those leaders accordingly. These beliefs are called prototypes. Often these prototypes are shaped by culture, history, and the media, and they're extremely resistant to change, even in the face of strong evidence. Furthermore, research shows how these prototypes can become socially conceived (agreed to by everyone) and shared between people. Add to this the fact that the popular press reinforces these beliefs by continually printing articles glorifying, or vilifying, singular leaders. (It's easier to report organizational outcomes by focusing on actions of the charismatic leader than to do in-depth investigative reporting. Does the term fake news sound familiar?)

Sadly, the vast majority of students also need to share some of the responsibility for the leadership disease, along with their complicit professors. They demand simplistic leadership models that they can memorize for a test, and they punish the professors who teach more-nuanced approaches to the art of influence by handing out poor teacher ratings.

Thus, there are many forces at play that reinforce the leadership-as-a-role perspective. That said, there are some strong historical roots for this perspective, and we believe that it's always useful to look to history before attempting to move forward. We explore these historical roots in the next chapter.

Chapter 2

∽

The Historical Roots of the
Leadership Disease

L ET'S GO BACK IN TIME to understand how we've arrived at this point, where the leadership disease is rampant in business, government, and non-profit organizations.

People began to formally study leadership during the beginning of the Industrial Revolution. Jean Baptiste Say, a French economist, for example, stated that entrepreneurs "must possess the art of supervision and administration." A major undertaking during the Industrial Revolution was the creation of railroads. These enterprises were geographically dispersed and necessitated the innovation and implementation of mechanisms to coordinate and manage the vast resources, human and otherwise, that were required. A prominent railroad executive of the era, Daniel C. McCallum, introduced six principles of management. One important principle that he wrote about, which is directly related to leadership, is unity of command – no subordinate should report to more than one boss – implying that leadership should come from the top and orders followed by those below. This initial thinking on leadership for industrial enterprise embedded the idea that centralized, top-down leadership was the best way to manage organizations.

Later, in the early 1900s, scientific management further reinforced the dominant views on management and leadership, suggesting that it flows in one direction, from the top down. In particular, it fostered the separation of responsibilities of managers and workers. Managers were responsible for identifying the best way to get things done, and workers were to obediently follow the prescriptions of management. The idea that subordinates could have a role in the process of leadership was unthinkable.

To illustrate this point, Peter Drucker – the Father of Modern Management – recalled a conversation he had with a friend of his who worked at the National Labor Relations Board in the 1940s. When Drucker mentioned the notion that labor and management had some common interests, his friend retorted that any organization that suggested such a thing was prima facie in violation

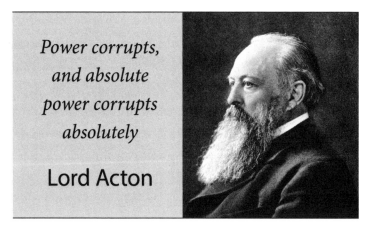

Power corrupts, and absolute power corrupts absolutely

Lord Acton

Figure 2. Lord Acton's quote exemplifies the essence of the leadership disease.

of labor law. The implication was that the leadership perspective of the day was as follows: there was to be a separation of power, with labor having power only over labor contracts, and it was the prerogative of management to tell labor what to do, within the confines of the labor contract. In other words, top-down leadership.

Today's leadership lexicon includes many terms, such as transactional, transformational, and empowering leadership, that describe apparent alternatives to the more autocratic leadership model of early industrial organizations. Nevertheless, the notion that leadership is something that primarily resides in a person or a relatively small set of people, and that it tends to flow downward, remains firmly ensconced in the vast majority of leadership training and development programs. To the extent that we continue to develop this persistent leadership model we allow the insidious, festering spread of the leadership disease. In the 1800s, Lord Acton summarized the essence of the leadership disease with his famous quote, "Power corrupts, and absolute power corrupts absolutely" (see Figure 2). We illuminate the terrible human outcomes of the leadership disease in chapter three.

Chapter 3

࿐

Manifestations of
the Leadership Disease

ADLY, A WIDE VARIETY OF DIRE OUTCOMES have resulted from misguided leadership practice. In fact, scandalous examples of leadership corruption and abuse of power have become so commonplace that there's a danger of being desensitized, accepting these practices as normal. Relatively recent organizational scandals and apparent ethical shortfalls that have rocked the business world include exploits at Adelphia, Countrywide, Enron, WorldCom, Tyco, Toyota, and British Petroleum, to name just a few organizations.

If we shift our view from organizations to nations, the impact of the leadership disease is far worse. The group of horribles is unfortunately very large. It includes the likes of Kim Jong-un of North Korea, inflicting suffering on the population of his country, while exercising his plump power. Of course, Syria's Bashar al-Assad is another no-nonsense, "it's all for me" despot, destroying his country just to keep his death grip on power. Then there's Jacob Zuma of South Africa, sinking the most developed country of the continent into an abyss. But disgusting dictators are not limited to just a few countries. Examples such as these are commonplace, to the point that identifying yet additional ethical failures by leaders has almost become cliché.

In the more extreme cases of the leadership disease, high-profile leaders with thousands of employees in their companies, or millions of citizens in their countries, have made incredibly poor decisions that have demonstrated dramatic abuses of power, clearly exposing deeply corrupt values. Subsequently, embezzlement, obfuscation, and self-serving actions at the expense of others have emerged as symbols of what leaders, given the opportunity for exploitation, simply do.

High-profile leaders falling from grace is also all too commonplace in today's organizational landscape. Leaders such as Sanjay Kumar (Computer Associates), Andy Fastow (Enron), and Bernie Madoff (Madoff Investment Securities) have been sentenced to prison for their diabolical deeds, especially fraud.

Corruption, of course, is a global concern that extends well beyond the borders of the United States. Let's look at Nigeria. The entire country is in desperate shape because of rampant corruption. One governor after another has been nabbed for corruption, and it doesn't end with them. What's truly sad about Nigeria is that, while the population cries out against corruption, many people call their leaders who don't take advantage of their position to line their own pockets mugus, a term used to describe incredibly stupid people. Thus, while many Nigerians decry corruption, they also wish that they could be in a position to engage in, and prosper from, corruption. Is it any wonder why Nigeria is in such dire straights?

For our purpose here we rely on the leadership disease metaphor to capture the scope and perniciousness of this problem. The manifestations of this disease include corruption, when leaders engage in unethical acts; abuse of power, when leaders use their power and influence for personal gain at the expense of others; and the waste of human potential, when leaders only consider their own outcomes. This last manifestation encompasses two aspects: workers not being able to intellectually contribute at work and the loss of jobs and opportunities that employees and citizens endure when leaders drive companies and countries to the brink of destruction in their pursuit of misplaced goals. Together these manifestations of the leadership disease epitomize what we call socially irresponsible leadership.

On the one hand, there has been an increasing focus on topics such as corporate social responsibility (CSR) all around the world. On the other hand, corporate social ir-responsibility (CSIR) is also on the rise. There's even evidence that some leaders, after engaging in CSR, feel that they have a moral license to engage in CSIR – they rationalize that if they did something good it's okay to do something bad, since "I'm a good guy." CSIR takes many forms, including wasting human talent, seeking personal gain at the expense of other stakeholders, and even outright corruption. It's the absolute antithesis of CSR. It typically involves unethical behavior that demonstrates disregard for others' welfare, and, in the extreme, is manifested when leaders seek wanton personal gain at the expense of employees, shareholders, and other organization stakeholders, and even society at large. The many recent cases of top executive corruption and misuse of power have put the spotlight on CSIR as a major challenge for human resource management thought and practice in the 21st century.

Top executives aren't the only source of CSIR. Destructive acts can occur in organizations and governments at any level, and these individual acts add up. But we've focused mostly on executives and high-ranking officials because they're in positions that enable more profound effects.

Naturally, researchers are studying why corruption and CSIR flourish. From philosophy we learn that standards for moral behavior are important in all facets of human life, which isn't surprising. The field of psychology, however, provides greater insight into the fine-grained mechanisms that can activate CSIR. Cognitive moral development (someone's level of moral reasoning), locus of control (the degree to which someone thinks they can control events), and Machiavellianism (when someone believes that any means, however immoral, can justifiably be used in achieving power), each of which are detectable through psychological testing, are all predictors of engagement in corruption and CSIR. The influence of leadership on CSIR – particularly when we look at executive-level leadership – is something we need to take very seriously.

Corruption and CSIR aren't new. Surveys of *Harvard Business Review* readers in 1961 and 1977 revealed that the behavior of one's immediate supervisor was the factor ranked highest when it came to unethical decision making. More-contemporary research has specifically documented how leaders play a major role in the institutionalization of corruption because they're role models for those below them in the hierarchy. These higher-level leaders can effectively ignore, condone, or even reward corrupt behavior. Leaders, especially those at higher levels, are essentially in a position to authorize corruption. Because CSIR-type activities have such a profound effect, they require ever more scrutiny in order to find ways to safeguard all of us.

Different terms – including antisocial behavior, delinquency, anti-citizenship behavior, deviance and corruption – have been employed to depict types of behavior related to CSIR. With that said, most of the research on such behavior in organizations has been conducted in the lower levels of organizations, where their effects are generally far less extreme than when they're sanctioned organization-wide.

Research on employee sabotage, theft, retaliation, litigation, aggression, and even anti-social humor has documented an unfortunately high amount of such activity. These deviant behaviors, naturally, bring about detrimental effects on organizations. The important thing to note, however, is that the primary driving force of these organizational outcomes appears to be offensive or abusive leader behavior: Destructive criticism from a leader causes people to feel anger and tension and to engage in resistance and avoidance – and it hurts their performance. When leaders use harsh discipline, people engage in more anti-citizenship behavior; when people perceive exploitation or provocation, they engage in more aggressiveness; when leaders act like petty tyrants, organizations experience bizarre dysfunction; and, finally, when leaders micro-manage, people engage in more complaining, defiance, absenteeism, and work avoidance.

Now THAT WE'VE IDENTIFIED the leadership disease, we'll turn our attention to providing an overview of the various influence options available to leaders for engaging others.

Chapter 4

≈

Four Common Approaches to Leadership Practice

THE TRADITIONAL PRACTICE OF LEADERSHIP has been categorized according to four specific leadership approaches (or leader behaviors), which have been clearly identified through much research (see Figure 3). Most often these common leadership approaches have been studied assuming a hierarchical leader perspective – where designated leaders lead and followers follow. In this book, however, we expand on this perspective by recognizing that different organizational or societal members (whether they're formally designated as leaders or not) can exercise leadership when their distinct skills or knowledge are needed at various points in a social process.

First, we'll summarize these four leadership approaches. Later (in Chapter Seven) we'll examine some specific practices that are needed from hierarchical leaders to help support the ongoing development of the effective leadership potential of various other organizational members. In reality, effective leadership must recognize that the agents and targets of influence are often peers.

Figure 3 demonstrates the science behind our common leadership approaches – directive, transactional, transformational, and super (empowering) leadership – that people have been shown to use in influencing others. Research has clearly identified that these four major types of leader behavior can emanate from hierarchical leaders or be shared and distributed among subordinates, followers, or peers. Each of these leadership approaches is described in more detail below. It's important to note that each of these approaches to leadership has pros and cons. We describe when to deploy each approach, as well as the potential liabilities of each approach, in Figure 4. Note that leaders can exhibit any or all of these behaviors, depending on circumstances.

Directive Leader Behavior

Directive leader behavior involves providing task-focused direction, as the term implies. Directive leadership is very important, for instance, for those new to a position, who necessarily require direction. Directive leader behavior

Primary Approaches to Leadership

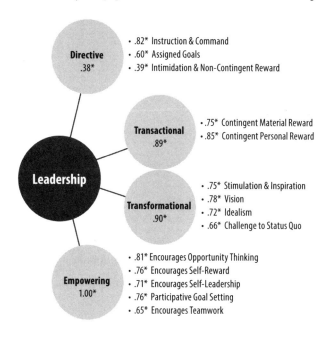

Figure 3. Scientific research has clearly identified the primary approaches to leadership, shown in the gray circles. The bulleted items are specific behaviors associated with each type of leadership. The numbers are factor loadings (similar to correlations) from a confirmatory factor analysis (a sophisticated statistical technique for analyzing leader behavior). The asterisks indicate that all of the loadings are scientifically significant.

helps to provide clarity for unclear tasks. Highly skilled individuals, be they designated leaders or not, will generally find a receptive audience in less-knowledgeable or

PROS AND CONS OF LEADER BEHAVIORS

Leader Behavior	When/Why to Deploy	Potential Liabilities
Directive	• When individuals are new • When others are not skilled at the task • For immediate actions (e.g., the building is on fire)	• Limits development of followers • Places large burden on the leader • Limits amount of information considered
Transactional	• Rational maintenance leadership • For exemplary performance • For social celebration of contributions	• Creates over emphasis on "extrinsic" motivation • Narrows focus of followers' work to those things that are explicitly rewarded
Transformational	• Provides focus on overarching goals • Enables people to fill in the blanks between specific tasks • Encourages citizenship behavior • Facilitates resilience in the face of setbacks	• Is confounded with narcissism – followers need to be careful to evaluate the sincerity of the leader • Can grow tiresome if overdone for trivial tasks
Super (Empowering)	• Is focused on development of others • Creates higher levels of ownership • Creates higher levels of motivation • Creates higher levels of commitment	• Often leaders empower others without clearly specifying boundaries – boundaries must be clear • People must be capable and responsible with empowerment – not everyone can be trusted to receive empowerment

Figure 4. Each of the four approaches to leadership demonstrates pros and cons, and leaders can exhibit any of these behaviors.

less-experienced people for benevolent and constructive directions and instructions. Directive leader behavior is especially important in newly created groups or teams. For example, shared directive leadership can come into play when peers explore ideas with one another through a directive give-and-take about how to approach tasks, allocate roles, or resolve conflicting points of view. Of course, directive leadership is also quite important for tasks that require immediate action (e.g., the proverbial building-on-fire scenario).

There are some potential liabilities to directive leadership. For instance, if it's over-used in the relationship between a superior and subordinate, it truly stunts development. Moreover, it places a heavy burden on the nominal leader, and it limits the consideration of information that can come from more-inclusive approaches to leadership.

The recent Chief Executive Officer of Cisco, during the latter part of his tenure as CEO, began purposely striving to broaden participation in decision making and direction giving in the company's leadership process. Reflecting on the difficulties Cisco faced following the dot-bomb era, CEO John Chambers stated, "All decisions came to the top ten people in the company, and we drove things back down from there." Now Cisco uses a thoughtful strategy of engaging shared directive leadership, with fairly impressive results. According to Chambers, "The boards and councils [we created] have been able to innovate with tremendous speed. Fifteen minutes and one week to get a [business] plan that used to take six months!" By engaging the directive capabilities of a broader range of the organizational hierarchy, Cisco has been able to reap substantial rewards relative to their top-down, directive leadership-dependent competitors.

Transactional Leader Behavior

Transactional leader behavior is about exchange relationships. It's focused on providing rewards (praise, recognition, or remuneration) in exchange for desired behavior. While monetary rewards are generally reserved for hierarchical leadership relations, the other rewards can come from anybody – shared transactional leadership. With that said, from our consulting practice experiences we can report that some innovative organizations are experimenting with peer input on monetary rewards.

Transactional leader behavior is best characterized as rational maintenance leadership. We all like, and deserve, rewards. So it's important in social interactions to carefully consider recognizing and rewarding effective behavior, especially exemplary behavior, on the part of others, be they subordinates or peers. That's only rational. Likewise, it's critical to celebrate outstanding contributions or group success socially, helping to maintain the behavior. On the downside, transactional leader behavior can inadvertently cause people to behave only in ways that are explicitly rewarded, and this is especially true for monetary rewards. Psychologists have documented how this can actually decrease intrinsic motivation – people may do things to be rewarded rather than because they feel they are the right things to do. Thus, you need to be careful about overemphasizing rewards.

Transformational Leader Behavior

While transactional leader behavior emphasizes rewards that are of a more immediate nature, transformational leader behavior is more forward looking, with an emphasis on emotional engagement, commitment to a collective vision, and fulfillment of higher-order needs, such as creating meaning and having a sense of personal impact. One of the critical tasks of the hierarchical leader is to help provide a focus on the overarching vision, but subordinates, followers, and peers have an important role here as well. If a vision is to be shared, engagement of many people in the creation of the vision is, to say the least, helpful. Therefore, shared transformational leader behavior is critical. The deployment of transformational leader behavior enables people to fill in the gaps between otherwise clearly defined tasks associated with directive leadership. It also encourages citizenship behavior and facilitates resilience in the face of difficulties.

Of course, there are some potential pitfalls of transformational leader behavior. For example, transformational leaders, be they hierarchical leaders or from a group of one's peers, can have radically different motivations. Some people are truly concerned with the larger collective, while others use the ruse of transformational leadership to cover their narcissistic tendencies to crave attention. The difficulty here is the ability to discern the real motivations of those attempting to exert this type of influence. All we can say is, buyer beware – try to be observant of the underlying motivation of others appealing to (supposed) higher-level goals. Naturally, over-emphasis on such leadership can also become tiresome, especially for trivial tasks.

Shared transformational leadership, however, offers great potential to engage both employees and volunteers. We spoke with Leslie E. Stocker, former president of the Braille Institute of America, who claimed, "We all have a voice in creating our common mission . . . the key is to help others lead you when they have the relevant knowledge."

Super (Empowering) Leader Behavior

SuperLeadership is all about empowering others. We briefly review it here, but we'll expand on our discussion of SuperLeadership later in this book, in Chapter Seven. Like the other three basic approaches to leadership, SuperLeader behavior can come from a hierarchical leader or from others not in a hierarchical position of power. SuperLeadership helps to develop others, as well as to enhance ownership, motivation, and commitment. SuperLeadership concentrates on developing others' skills in self-management and self-leadership. One major mistake people make, however, when deploying SuperLeadership is to empower others without clearly establishing boundaries. It's also important to be certain that people are capable of engaging in the activities for which they're empowered. But more on SuperLeadership later.

Chapter 5

༂

Leadership Is a Process, Not Just a Role

THERE'S MORE TO EFFECTIVE LEADERSHIP, and to finding a cure for the all-to-widespread leadership disease, than simply becoming adept at using the common approaches to leadership – directive, transactional, transformational, and super (empowering) leader behaviors – to influence others. We have historically been taught that leadership is a role – that someone is the leader and the others are followers. But to achieve truly effective leadership, with and for everyone – that is, by using twisted leadership – we need to revise our understanding of leadership fairly substantially, and we need to view it as a dynamic, unfolding, complex social process (see Figure 5).

We need to make a very important distinction here: A manager is not always a leader. A manager has a role as

Leadership Is a Process

Figure 5. Leadership is a complex social process, and leaders can come from any level of an organization.

a supervisor of something: a project, function, people, or all of those things. He or she will have some degree of influence because of their role as a manager. However, a leader can appear from anywhere in an organization or community. Leaders develop influence because of who they are, and people follow them because they want to follow them. People can influence others because they have something that those others need and respect, such as expertise, experience, insight, creativity, or calm in the face of crisis.

This leadership perspective means that instead of just having to rely on one person to lead, any given group can exchange leadership dynamically, based on the context, project, goals, knowledge, experience, or general needs of the group. This then creates a power dynamic within a group that transcends a traditional hierarchy based on one person. Instead it builds on the sense of community that is innate in all societies. For the sake of simplicity, we call this perspective twisted leadership, which consists of the four strands of self-leadership, SuperLeadership, shared leadership, and socially responsible leadership. There have been instances of these strands of twisted leadership throughout history, but typically they've resulted by accident, organically, without conscious intent. Imagine the possible results you might see by intentionally harnessing the synergistic power of these four interconnected strands of leadership in your organization.

Today we know that twisted leadership can be built into organizations at their inception, or it can be inculcated over time if the organization is more mature. We know that if an organization or group decides to operate in a manner that encourages and enables, for example, shared leadership, it will become part of the DNA of that group. And the same goes for the three other strands of twisted leadership.

Part Two

჻

Effective Medications for the Leadership Disease

ELIMINATING THE LEADERSHIP DISEASE requires a significant shift in how we describe, frame, and prescribe leadership as an unfolding social process, as opposed to leadership simply as a role that's occupied by a specific individual. Developing this alternative approach to leadership involves a focus on four leadership medications that can help end the malignancy of the disease:

჻ **Self-leadership** – which largely explodes the notion of sheep-like followers by designating everyone as a leader . . . of themselves

჻ **SuperLeadership** – a practical, hierarchically connected approach to leadership that is centered on leading others to lead themselves and one another (to self-lead and share the lead)

- ⮞ **Shared leadership** – which describes how nearly every group member can play an important role in a dynamic, interactive leadership process

- ⮞ **Socially responsible leadership** – which connects leadership to a value base that's concerned with the welfare and needs of all stakeholders

THE PHILOSOPHY OF TWISTED LEADERSHIP is to engage, more broadly, the leadership potential of everyone (see Figure 6). Each of these four strands of leadership is described in more detail in the following chapters.

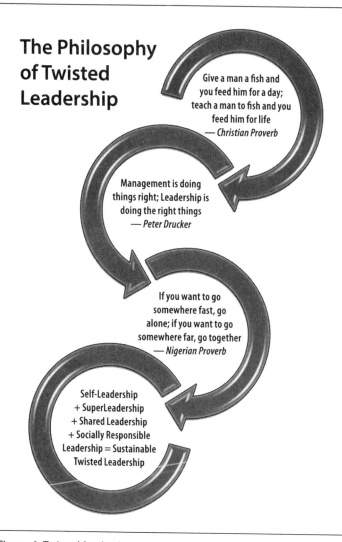

The Philosophy of Twisted Leadership

Give a man a fish and you feed him for a day; teach a man to fish and you feed him for life
— *Christian Proverb*

Management is doing things right; Leadership is doing the right things
— *Peter Drucker*

If you want to go somewhere fast, go alone; if you want to go somewhere far, go together
— *Nigerian Proverb*

Self-Leadership
+ SuperLeadership
+ Shared Leadership
+ Socially Responsible
Leadership = Sustainable
Twisted Leadership

Figure 6. Twisted leadership aims at engaging the leadership potential of everyone.

Chapter 6

ॐ

Self-Leadership (S1)

THE FOLLOWING POINTS provide a quick summary regarding the nature of self-leadership:

ॐ Views everyone as a leader . . . of themselves – a self-empowering leadership view that helps bring out the best in everyone

ॐ Recognizes the unique and valuable features of each person, and helps to enhance them

ॐ Unleashes each person's inner potential so that individual knowledge, experience, and capacities are more fully optimized

ॐ Helps create pillars of strength (capable and independent self-leaders) throughout organizations, as opposed to restricting leadership to a single person,

or a few people, who happen to be assigned a leadership role

  ~ Works well in environments with individual-based
jobs, but also supports collaborative work by equip-
ping team members to step forward and contribute
when they're needed, and step back (and get out of
the way) when the inputs of others are needed

  ~ When combined with shared leadership, offers
checks and balances ("We" vs. "Me") that can deter
corrupt/unethical behaviors as well as groupthink

You can and do lead yourself. So does everyone
else. But that doesn't mean that we're all good at self-
leadership, or that we couldn't improve significantly on
how well we lead ourselves. In fact, by applying inten-
tional and well-thought-out strategies, we can become
better self-leaders. And organizations can reap substantial benefits if they recognize and facilitate self-leadership
throughout their workforce as part of a broader twisted
leadership approach. Unfortunately, this often doesn't occur, since leadership is generally viewed in a different way
. . . again, sadly, consistent with the leadership disease.

Research and writing on leadership normally focuses
on people who are formally designated as leaders and on

Figure 7. All people can lead themselves, and there are numerous strategies that can be used that result in effective self-leadership.

how they influence progress toward goals. This view supports treating leadership as a centralized role that's restricted to people in formal, hierarchical positions. Despite this, people can, and do, lead themselves, every day. What's more, there's clear scientific evidence that people are able to engage in effective self-leadership, identifying the whys of their efforts, in addition to the whats and hows. Self-leadership (see Figure 7) occurs naturally but often not effectively, so developing self-leadership capacity and skill, and learning specific self-leadership strategies, is important. As we've said, leaders (and the influence they have on so-called followers) can be people other than those who are formally designated as leaders, raising a striking, and potentially much more optimal, alternative to a centralized, hierarchical perspective.

Originally, the concept of self-leadership, as it has been applied to work settings, was largely based on the self-control and self-management literature in clinical psychology. An example is the literature that's focused on people eliminating bad habits, such as overeating or smoking, often with a theme of supporting more disciplined choices. The literature on the expanded concept of self-leadership, especially applied to work situations, supports the idea that leadership doesn't require traditional leader and follower roles and can originate from the self. That is, a leader and follower can be the same person since influence is self-applied.

The concept of self-leadership suggests that all people can lead themselves, at least in part, and offers a potent twist on views that say leadership needs to be an outward process where people in leader roles influence others in follower roles. Such a self-influence view is typically not recognized, or it's ignored, in the framing of leadership, even in contexts heavily reliant on knowledge workers and/or employee empowerment and self-managing work teams. Recognizing the significance and potential contributions of self-leadership is an important part of sharing and distributing leadership throughout organizations. In the spectrum of approaches to participation and empowerment, self-leadership is an advanced form of self-influence. The concept of self-leadership incorporates and extends parts of other, earlier self-influence concepts such as self-management, i.e., managing ourselves via self-discipline-type strategies that focus on behavior in order to reach goals and standards, which are typically defined by others (for example, a formal leader or boss, or norms in society at large).

Self-leadership is not only concerned with influencing our behavior to reach current standards and goals, it also involves evaluating the legitimacy of the standards and changing them or setting different ones. That means it examines what's to be done and why, in addition to considering how to perform. Self-leadership concerns strategy as well as the natural or intrinsic rewards of task performance. Self-leadership directly challenges traditional views of leadership based on formal, authority-based hierarchies and leaders. That means that self-leadership can be at the heart of empowering employees and reducing the dependence-creating role of traditional leader authority figures.

Self-Leadership and Its Many Forms[1]

There are many kinds of self-leadership strategies, including those focused on behavior, natural rewards, and thoughts.

Behavioral-Focused Strategies

Behavioral-focused self-leadership strategies include self-observation, self-goal setting, self-reinforcement, and self-criticism. Self-observation – observing your behaviors to gain information about them – is critical for better understanding your motivations and tendencies. Self-goal setting helps direct and channel your effort by establishing targets to pursue. Self-reinforcement and self-punishment (or self-criticism) both rely on self-applied consequences for your actions (positive and negative). In general, each of these strategies has been found to support increased performance and other positive outcomes (except self-punishment, which can be demoralizing and otherwise ineffective) for many types of people, including employees, college students, and trainees.[2]

Research shows that behavioral-focused strategies are effective because self-observation increases self-awareness, which in turn creates a foundation for positive change via better choices and the application of other strategies. In general, effective self-leaders display increased effort and place more value on gaining self-awareness than others. Taking notes throughout the day about important events, journaling, and requesting feedback from coworkers or leaders are examples of the kind of self-observation strategies that self-leaders can use. As another example, behavioral-focused strategies can be used to support improved physical health, better stamina, and overall wellbeing. In this regard, self-leadership strategies might include setting fitness goals, reinforcing your motivation for physical exercise, and using relaxation techniques such as deep breathing and meditation.

Natural Reward Strategies

Self-leadership strategies can also focus on promoting positive feelings. The key is to connect with your work in a way that motivates you to perform a task because you naturally want to do it for its own value, rather than for something you receive (a reward) that's separate from the task. Natural reward self-leadership strategies involve focusing on and building in naturally motivating features of work activities. That is, you can practice an important part of self-leadership by redesigning your tasks, and/or how you think about them, in ways that help you feel more competence, self-control, and/or purpose. Also, when your goals and naturally motivating tasks are consistent with your personal wellbeing and values, you can reinforce your feelings of purpose.

Even seemingly menial jobs can be reinterpreted in ways that are more uplifting by using strategies that expand duties and add purpose and meaning.[3] For example, research shows that for otherwise unappealing activities, such as nurses bathing patients, a more positive relationship to the task can be established by intentionally focusing on valued features that provide meaning and purpose, in this case trying to increase the comfort of patients.[4]

Constructive Thought Strategies

Constructive thought strategies are designed to influence the focus and nature of your thoughts to make them more productive. Strategies include influencing the focus of your mental imagery, your self-talk, and your assumptions and beliefs, and combining these foci to establish overall thinking patterns. For example, research indicates that by replacing dysfunctional mental imagery, self-talk, and/or assumptions and beliefs with more constructive thoughts you can increase your self-efficacy (confidence that you can successfully perform specific activities), persistence, and use and accomplishment of challenging self-goals. And all this can help you be more effective in general.

Many contexts have been used for conducting research on thought self-leadership. The overall findings are that thought self-leadership can promote thought processes and mental attention that support constructive thinking patterns and habits. The bottom line is that thought self-leadership can have positive effects ranging from productivity to enhanced learning to career success.

Higher-Level Self-Leadership

Before we turn our attention to SuperLeadership (our next S), it's useful to consider ways that self-leadership can support social responsibility, or what we call the self-leadership high road (see Figure 8). This high road has three primary components – responsibility, authenticity, and expanded capacity.

- ❧ **Responsibility** – This component focuses on self-led intentions and behaviors related to being responsible. Similar to corporate social responsibility

The Self-Leadership High Road

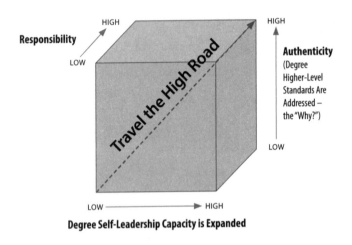

Degree Self-Leadership Capacity is Expanded

Figure 8. You move further along the self-leadership high road by increasing your responsibility, authenticity, and expanded capacity.

and virtue, the concern here is for the wider good (employees, citizens, members of the international community, and stakeholders in general) as part of self-leadership. Virtue, for example, reflects concern with higher-level values (such as courage, compassion, integrity), that is, values with a transcendent purpose.

ೞ **Authenticity** – This component centers on the role of higher-level standards that guide behavior. Here we're concerned with questions regarding what you will do and, especially, why you will do it that go beyond the more basic questions concerning how you will do it. The heart of authenticity in self-leadership involves the primary reasons for behaving a certain way and how consistent those reasons are with your personal values. This contrasts with ceding the rationale for your self-influence to other sources, such as a boss or company norms and values.

☙ **Expanded capacity** – This component deals with self-leadership strategies and methods that contribute to a wider range of self-leadership capacities, which in turn can contribute to the potential of the previous two components. Expanded self-leadership capacity can better enable self-leaders to pursue authentic choices and behaviors as well as choose responsible ends. Expanded capacity can and should involve adding skills in newer and less developed areas; for example, it might include self-leadership of fitness and health, emotion, and collaboration/teamwork with others, if these areas have been relatively neglected. Expanded capacity goes beyond simply increasing your mastery and practice of self-leadership strategies that you already know and use well.

The three primary components of the self-leadership high road are shown in the three-dimensional model in Figure 8. When each of the three components is increased – more emphasis on responsibility (as opposed to irresponsibility), greater authenticity through more attention to higher standards, and expanded capacity – you move further along the self-leadership high road in terms of self-leadership practice.

All this means that optimal self-leadership can involve more than simply leading yourself to high performance. It can be deeply rooted in a self-led life and career that's authentic, responsible, and includes continuous learning and expansion of your capacities.

The way that self-leadership is put into practice will differ from person to person, depending on each person's unique nature, perspectives, motivations, etc. That said, an example of a fairly comprehensive self-leadership system can be summarized with seven steps to self-leadership (see Figure 9).

Seven Steps to Self-Leadership

Step 1: Get to know yourself better.

Observe and study yourself – your interests, strengths and weaknesses, primary motivations, etc. Track your current

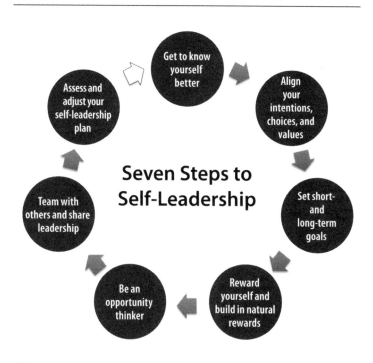

Figure 9. These seven steps to self-leadership will help you create an effective self-leadership system.

choices and their results. You might chart the frequency and trends of key behaviors, thoughts, and emotions that you find of particular interest or importance. You could graph these results over time or keep a journal. The better you know yourself the better equipped you'll be to develop and apply a self-leadership plan and set of strategies well suited to you.

Step 2: Align your intentions and choices with your deepest values as a foundation for authentic self-leadership practice.

Supported by Step 1, identify the values that are most central for you. Ask yourself what aspects of your life and work provide you with the greatest sense of purpose and meaning. Work to align your self-leadership approach and specific strategies with what you value most. Use this step as a foundation for Step 3 – setting your self-leadership goals.

Step 3: Set short- and long-term goals.

Set specific, challenging, but achievable goals for both the short and long term. Unless you pay special attention to targeting effective choices in the form of specific self-goals, it's very difficult to consistently follow through with practical, performance-enhancing practices. For example, commit to thirty minutes of developmental reading each day in new, important knowledge areas. You might also set a goal to take a brisk twenty-to-thirty-minute walk each day to promote clearer thinking and better stamina. And establish specific, long-term career goals as well, such as identifying the kind of achievements and job positions you aspire to in your career.

Step 4: Reward yourself and build natural rewards into your activities.

Build self-rewards into your self-leadership system to help increase your motivation. As you progress and reach your shorter-term goals, reward yourself with things you like and value (nice dinners out, travel, enjoyable activities). You might also provide yourself with constructive, critical feedback in areas you think you need to improve. In addition, focus on and build natural rewards into your activities and tasks. Redesign tasks to better fit your natural interests and strengths.

Step 5: Be an opportunity thinker and create positive thought patterns (habits).

Practice thinking constructively and positively – focus on opportunities rather than retreating from obstacles. Look for the opportunities nested in your daily challenges rather than focusing on all the reasons to give up and stop trying. Also, try to better recognize your own potential and capabilities for being an innovative high performer – believe in yourself. Much of your success or failure in progressing toward strong performance and a great career depends on the way you think about yourself. Remind yourself that every slip, error, or falling short on a specific task can provide an opportunity for exploring how your personalized self-leadership program can be further adjusted and improved for future success.

Step 6: Increase your self-leadership through teaming with others and sharing leadership.

Strive to work with, support, and be supported by your colleagues. When you commit to working collaboratively with others, and you and your colleagues encourage and reinforce one another, you amplify your potential success. Teams and shared leadership can be a crucial part of effective self-leadership – through teamwork and shared leadership you can multiply your potential well beyond your own personal limitations, since no one can know everything and be accomplished in all skill areas. If you choose to work with others with a team orientation, a solid foundation for increased learning, performance, and potential improvement can be established.

Step 7: Assess and adjust your self-leadership plan and approach as needed.

Examine and assess your ongoing self-leadership practices. Add new self-leadership strategies that you think are needed and will be helpful, eliminate those that simply aren't working, and adjust those that are helping but need improvement. Overall, emphasize what's working or might work for you and reduce what's not. Continuously customize your self-leadership approach with the intent of better aligning your results with your deepest values and in ways that offer the most promise for optimal outcomes. Return to Step 1 and continue to refine your self-leadership system.

Time to Reflect

Reflect for a moment. Have you ever systematically thought about how you lead yourself? What kind of specific self-leadership strategies can you think of that you've used (keeping to-do lists, setting goals for yourself, etc.)? Consider writing down some thoughts about how you've practiced self-leadership in the past and how you might improve on it going forward. How could self-leadership help you to lead yourself to a healthier, more-effective career and life? Study the strategies of self-leadership. Which of them have you used effectively in the past? Which of them should you work on so that you could use them more effectively? Finally, if you were going to modify the seven steps to better fit with your unique needs and motivations, how would you rewrite them? Consider taking a few minutes to rewrite them now.

A PLACE TO RECORD YOUR THOUGHTS

Have you thought about how you lead yourself?

What self-leadership strategies have you used?

How have you practiced self-leadership in the past?

How might you improve on it going forward?

How could self-leadership help you to lead yourself to a healthier, more-effective career and life?

Which self-leadership strategies have you used effectively in the past?

Which strategies should you work on so that you could use them more effectively?

If you were going to modify the seven steps to better fit with your unique needs and motivations, how would you rewrite them?

Chapter 7

૭

SuperLeadership (S2)

HE FOLLOWING POINTS provide a quick summary regarding the nature of SuperLeadership:

- ૭ A highly empowering leadership approach that leads others to lead themselves

- ૭ Serves as a catalyst for self-leadership and shared leadership

- ૭ Supports and helps develop a team/collaborative context where commitment (going above and beyond), not just compliance, is desired

- ૭ Best applied when urgency isn't high because it can take time to employ – helps reduce crisis and urgency in the future by strengthening others' capacities to be proactive problem solvers and leaders of themselves and one another

~ Unleashes synergistic potential as knowledge, experience, and capacities are tapped from all involved

~ Spreads power and influence and counteracts the tendency for leaders to act as "self-kingmakers"

~ Facilitates the checks and balances ("We" vs. "Me") of self-leadership and shared leadership that can deter corrupt/unethical behaviors as well as groupthink

SUPERLEADERSHIP – sometimes referred to as empowering leadership – is an approach that centers on bringing out others' inner leadership capabilities as well as their best efforts. In this sense, being "Super" isn't based on our own capacities and limitations, but rather enables us as leaders to have the power of multitudes, because that power is based on unleashing the abilities, knowledge, and overall potential of others (see Figure 10).

Other types of leadership influence can be used to produce favorable results, at least for a time. But long-term problems and unintended side effects such as weakness and dependence can be created as well. Directive leaders influence by using a blunt, controlling approach. Transactional leaders influence by relying on

SuperLeadership

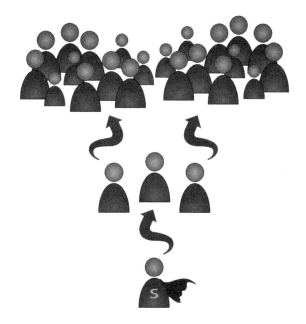

Figure 10. SuperLeadership unleashes the potential of others by empowering them to lead themselves.

a carrot (reward) and, sometimes, a stick (punishment). Both of these types of leaders generate compliance (a willingness to do the minimum that's asked for, but usually little more). In contrast, transformational leaders create above-and-beyond-the-call-of-duty commitment

Traditional Leadership	SuperLeadership
<ul><li>People are followers or subordinates</li><li>Power is the prerogative of the top leader</li><li>A leader's primary responsibility is to create the strategies, visions, plans, and instructions</li><li>Leaders are the source of wisdom</li></ul>	<ul><li>People are self-leaders</li><li>Power is shared</li><li>A leader's primary responsibility is to develop others and coordinate efforts</li><li>Wisdom is infused throughout all knowledge workers</li></ul>

Figure 11. Distinguishing features of traditional leadership versus SuperLeadership.

based on the leader's vision and inspiration. Yet all three of these leadership approaches, while useful at times in some situations, are leader-centric and can hinder self-leadership development and create follower dependence. This is not the case with SuperLeadership. Figure 11 describes the features of SuperLeadership that distinguish it from other types of leadership.

SuperLeaders empower others to lead themselves. They foster independence and interdependent teamwork (including shared leadership) and a deep sense of responsible commitment based on psychological ownership and purpose. The SuperLeadership approach was developed to fit with the challenges of contemporary leadership in today's complex, rapidly changing, and increasingly knowledge-based world. In many challenging situations,

Science Supports SuperLeadership

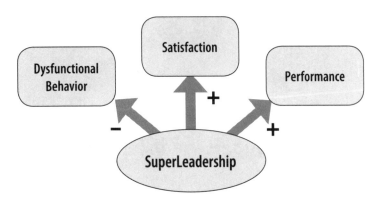

Figure 12. Research shows that SuperLeadership reduces dysfunctional behavior while increasing employee satisfaction and performance. Source: Vecchio, R., Justin, J., and Pearce, C. L. 2010. "Empowering Leadership." *Leadership Quarterly* 21(3): 530–42.

SuperLeadership can be used to help others with their own personal development. In fact, it can be the critical component for establishing a comprehensive, healthy leadership culture throughout an organization. By serving as an example and encouraging and reinforcing followers for taking responsibility, showing initiative, solving their own problems, and working effectively with others, a leader can become a SuperLeader. The scientific evidence for SuperLeadership is clear – it works (see Figure 12).

Figure 13. These seven steps to SuperLeadership will help you become an effective SuperLeader.

Seven Steps to SuperLeadership

Becoming a SuperLeader simply requires commitment. Nearly anyone can master the steps to SuperLeadership. The key parts of putting SuperLeadership into practice can be summarized in seven steps (see Figure 13).

Step 1: Become an effective self-leader.

The first step to becoming a SuperLeader is to become a better self-leader. The more effective you are in leading yourself, the more likely others will follow in your footsteps. Start by observing and learning more about yourself, and then set specific, challenging, but achievable goals. Reward yourself for your progress and accomplishments. You can also redesign aspects of your life and work to make them more enjoyable while still meeting your responsibilities. For example, redesign tasks to better fit your natural interests and strengths. Also, practice thinking constructively and positively with a focus on opportunities rather than retreating from obstacles.

Step 2: Model self-leadership for others.

Once you've mastered some self-leadership strategies, vividly display these effective techniques for your followers to see and learn from. Demonstrate self-leadership strategies in a clear and credible manner, and give followers (self-leaders) a chance to try them and to adapt them to their own needs. When others see you clearly introducing personalized, effective self-leadership practices into your daily routine and openly expressing the priority you place on them, they will have a live model to encourage them to consider their own work choices. For example, by sponsoring a pizza lunch (with colleagues who bring out the best in you) to discuss current challenges when you need others' insights (and when you want to have an enjoyable and motivating event) you can demonstrate your commitment to creative self-leadership strategies that enlist help and support from colleagues.

Step 3: Encourage others to set their own goals.

Unless special attention is devoted to targeting specific goals, it's very difficult to consistently follow through with practical performance-enhancing practices. Help followers learn the importance of setting challenging but realistic targets for their own performance and development – for example, by identifying a specific task to complete by a specific date, or, as suggested in the previous chapter, by committing to take a brisk twenty-to-thirty-minute walk each day to promote clearer thinking and better stamina. At first you can help them set their goals, and later you can gradually allow them to set their goals for themselves.

Step 4: Facilitate positive thought patterns.

Help followers to see their own potential and capabilities for being innovative high performers. Encourage them to believe in themselves and to look for the opportunities nested in their daily challenges, rather than focusing on all the reasons to give up and stop trying. Much of the success or failure in progressing toward strong performance and a great career depends on the way people think. Mistakes and setbacks can provide opportunities for helping your followers (self-leaders) explore how they can adjust their self-leadership practices, and the ways they collaborate with others, for future success.

Step 5: Reward self-leadership (and facilitate constructive critical feedback).

Recognize and reward followers for using self-leadership strategies and taking initiative and greater responsibility. Shift the focus of praise and rewards to effective self-leadership rather than focusing only on performance. As so-called followers transition toward being more-confident self-leaders, they should be able to better accept constructive, critical feedback focused on ways to further improve. And make sure that the critical feedback is constructive. Over time, those you are leading should grow in their capacity to provide constructive feedback for themselves.

Step 6: Promote team-oriented self-leadership and shared leadership.

Encouraging followers to work together and help one another is also very important. When people commit to working together and to encouraging and reinforcing one another, the potential for success can be improved significantly. Facilitating teams and shared leadership is a crucial part of SuperLeadership. As individuals are encouraged and reinforced, and as they ultimately proactively choose to work collaboratively and share influence, a solid foundation for a high-performance system of leadership and increasing success is established.

Step 7: Facilitate a culture of self-leadership and shared leadership.

Facilitate establishment of values and norms centered on self-leadership and shared leadership. When the first six steps to SuperLeadership are effectively performed, this final step should occur naturally. Encourage, guide, and reward initiative and responsibility. Also, in your own actions, continually demonstrate effective self-leadership and shared leadership that promote long-term progress and improvement. Eventually organization members should grow to recognize that it's not only okay to take initiative and responsibility, it's expected, and that taking those steps is the foundation of success in their organization.

IN SUMMARY, a SuperLeader is not an all-powerful leader but, instead, an empowering leader who: (1) leads others to lead themselves; (2) achieves long-term, sustainable results by tapping into the leadership potential in every person; (3) enables followers to stand on their own two feet and address, fix, and prevent problems whether the leader is around or not; and (4) creates independence (via self-leadership) and interdependence (via shared leadership). SuperLeadership causes followers to become:

- Motivated from the inside and to believe in themselves

- Deeply committed based on a sense of psychological ownership

- Independent and interdependent thinkers who pursue continuous improvement

- Self-leaders who are no longer followers

- Shared leaders who effectively share influence with each other

Time to Reflect

Take a moment to consider your own approach to leadership. Have you ever served as a SuperLeader to others? Your coworkers? Your children or other relatives? Consider writing down some of your thoughts on how and when you did this. Also, how might you use SuperLeadership to help others to lead themselves to a healthier, more-effective career and life going forward? Study the seven steps to SuperLeadership. Which of the steps have you used effectively in the past? Which steps do you need to work on to be able to use them more effectively for promoting self-leadership and shared leadership in others?

A PLACE TO RECORD YOUR THOUGHTS

Have you ever served as a SuperLeader to others? Who?

How and when did you do this?

How might you use SuperLeadership to help others?

Which of the steps to SuperLeadership have you used effectively?

Which steps to SuperLeadership do you need to improve?

Chapter 8

❧

Shared Leadership (S3)

HE FOLLOWING POINTS provide a quick summary regarding the nature of shared leadership:

- ❧ A comprehensive leadership view consisting of a continuous, simultaneous, mutual-influence process involving the serial emergence of various leaders who are both official and unofficial

- ❧ Includes the following classic leadership influence approaches – directive, transactional, transformational, and empowering

- ❧ Works best in team/collaborative contexts that involve interdependence and lower urgency and require creativity and employee commitment

  ⮞ Creates synergistic potential as knowledge, experience, and capacities are applied when they are needed

  ⮞ Can counteract potential self-serving biases

  ⮞ Combined with self-leadership, offers checks and balances ("We" vs. "Me") that can deter corrupt/unethical behaviors as well as groupthink

EMPOWERING PEOPLE to be more responsible for their own influence certainly has a role in helping to decentralize leadership, but shared leadership goes even further by helping to establish checks and balances in the overall leadership system. This results in a more dynamic, flexible, and robust leadership infrastructure (see Figure 14). Even though shared leadership is a fairly new scientific concept, there have been quite a few rigorous studies of it. The initial evidence, across a wide array of settings, shows that shared leadership has a powerful effect on various outcomes in both groups and organizations, as discussed below.

Shared leadership has a strong impact on group dynamics and performance. It's been shown to increase teamwork, courtesy, altruism, and a sense of resiliency, while reducing social loafing. Figure 15 illustrates the

Shared Leadership

Influence
Responsibility

Figure 14. Shared leadership means that various official and unofficial leaders emerge simultaneously within a group or organization. Responsibility and influence are shared among a set of individuals who lead each other toward goal achievement.

findings on shared leadership in a study of teams involved in developing innovation projects.

Importantly, shared leadership is a better predictor of group outcomes than is hierarchical leadership . . . and it flies in the face of any number of pop gurus' pseudo-sage advice (which is not based on science). This is an ideal time for a public service announcement: It's critical

Science Supports Shared Leadership

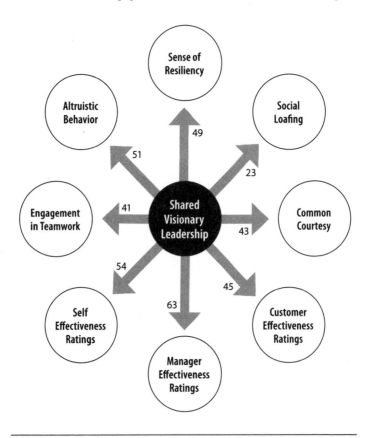

Figure 15. Research shows that shared visionary leadership increases a variety of desired behaviors including teamwork, courtesy, altruism, and a sense of resiliency while reducing social loafing. Source: Pearce, C. L. and Ensley, M. D. 2003. "A Reciprocal and Longitudinal Investigation of the Innovation Process." *Journal of Organizational Behavior* 25(2): 259–78.

to ascertain the veracity of the advice you follow – is it based on science or is it an unfounded opinion? To date, four studies have directly compared the effects of decentralized, shared leadership to the effects of centralized, hierarchical leadership, on several key group outcomes. In a study of change management teams, for instance, shared leadership was a better predictor of team effectiveness than hierarchical leadership, as rated by team members, managers above the teams, and customers of the teams. Shared leadership was also more effective than centralized, hierarchical leadership in ameliorating the dysfunctional influence of anti-citizenship behavior.

Shared leadership is also very effective in virtual teams, which are an ever-increasing aspect of organizational life. Shared leadership was a better predictor than hierarchical leadership of several important team outcomes, including problem-solving quality.

Perhaps most importantly, shared leadership is a strong predictor of organizational performance. In fact, a couple of studies – of *Inc.* 500 firms and small businesses – clearly document that shared leadership in top management teams is a better predictor of the financial performance of firms than Chief Executive Officer (CEO) leadership. Taken together, these studies demonstrate that shared leadership can provide a more robust leadership system than mere reliance on centralized, hierarchical leadership, including mitigating against CSIR.

Shared Leadership and Its Many Forms

Shared leadership is not a one-size-fits-all solution – it can take many forms. The four most common forms are: rotated shared leadership, integrated shared leadership, distributed shared leadership, and comprehensive shared leadership (see Figure 16). Below we describe each of these four forms, in some detail, to give you a feel for how shared leadership might best fit into your particular organizational circumstances.

Rotated Shared Leadership

Rotated shared leadership, as the term suggests, involves conscious strategies to have different people in a group clearly assume the role of leader at different times. This might be as simple as someone in a group agreeing to be a designated leader for a certain term with the understanding that the role will rotate to different members of the group at different times. Or another example: following something like *Robert's Rules of Order* for meetings involves quicker leadership transitions, where specific

Forms of Shared Leadership

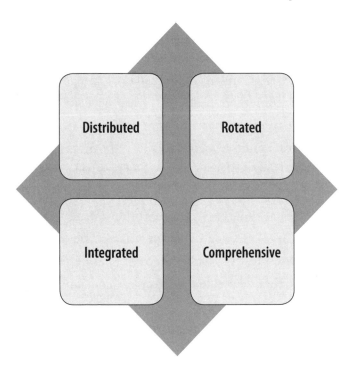

Figure 16. Shared leadership can take many forms – which one is appropriate for you depends on your particular circumstances.

rules determine when and how a person gets to take the floor as a leader. Rotated shared leadership is the simplest form of shared leadership, but it's a useful stepping stone to the more complex forms that follow.

One organization that has had great success with ro-tated shared leadership is Alcoholics Anonymous (AA). AA is a completely volunteer organization with a funda-mentally altruistic mission. It is focused on helping peo-ple who have historically been irresponsible self-leaders to heal, develop, and ultimately claim true personal re-sponsibility for their past and future decisions and ac-tions. The fundamental structure of AA is designed to offer participants a personalized interpretation of a structured process (Twelve Steps), where people can and do shift between the steps of that process as dictated by their personal situations. However, they are also told that their outcomes are solely their own responsibility.

In addition to the Twelve Steps of AA are the Twelve Traditions that delineate the manner that shared respon-sible leadership should be deployed within and among AA groups. The Traditions include: "Our common wel-fare should come first; personal recovery depends upon AA unity . . . Our leaders are but trusted servants; they do not govern . . . Each group should be autonomous except in matters affecting other groups or AA as a whole . . . Every AA group ought to be fully self-supporting, de-clining outside contributions . . . Alcoholics Anonymous should remain forever non-professional." AA is clearly an example of the rotated shared leadership model, and there are some unique leadership lessons to be gleaned from their example.

Integrated Shared Leadership

Southwest Airlines is an excellent example of integrated shared leadership. Southwest has shown a remarkable financial track record: If you invested $10,000 in Southwest Airlines in 1972 your investment would be worth well over $10,000,000 today. Southwest attributes its success to taking a more-balanced stakeholder perspective. They are one of the most admired companies in the United States, number seven according to the 2016 Fortune magazine rating. Fortune also rated Southwest as one of the top five best companies to work for. Southwest is regularly in the top of both categories. Ironically, however, the company doesn't achieve these high ratings by focusing on its financials or customers. Rather, Southwest achieves them by responsibly focusing on its employees. According to Jim Parker, former CEO of Southwest, "Many people think that the source of our success is our pay structure – that we pay our people less than our competitors – but that simply isn't true. The real source of our competitive advantage is our culture, which is based firmly on the principles of . . . shared leadership." Southwest shows how it's possible to achieve economic and strategic performance and sustainable growth through an integrated stakeholder approach to responsible leadership. The company is a contrast to the much more economically oriented approaches of many of its peers, in an industry that's been characterized by boom and bust and many large bankruptcies.

Distributed Shared Leadership

Distributed shared leadership, in contrast, deals more with how to disperse leadership roles more broadly in an organization. Shared leadership has enabled dramatic responsible leadership change to occur in a variety of places around the globe. For instance, the School Management Committees (SMCs) in Afghanistan have enabled shared leadership to flourish, leading to a radical shift in the leadership and governance of the country's education system. It's an example of distributed shared leadership in one of the most demanding environments you can imagine, and it enables the youth of a war-torn country to develop as the future leaders of their nation.

Megachurches, with their high-profile charismatic leaders, offer another glimpse into the potential for distributed shared leadership. While these leaders are often so arresting that their churches are accused of being cults of personality (and there's some truth to this, particularly in some of the newer megachurches), there's a distinct link between the sustainability and growth of these churches and their leaders' use and level of shared leadership. There are several prominent megachurch pastors who are quick to attribute the successes of their ministries to the distribution and sharing of leadership, including Rick Warren of Saddleback Church, Lake Forest, California; Joel Osteen of Lakewood Church, Houston, Texas; and Bill Hybels of Willow Creek Community Church, South Barrington, Illinois. A closer look at the style of leadership practiced in many megachurches that have sustainable growth, effective outreach ministries, and fewer scandals reveals at least some level of shared leadership as part of their management foundation.

Comprehensive Shared Leadership

Comprehensive shared leadership is present when sharing leadership is inculcated throughout many or all of the operations in an organization. Panda Restaurant Group, owner of Panda Express and other restaurant chains, is an exemplar of comprehensive shared leadership.

Panda Restaurant Group's stated mission is to "Deliver exceptional Asian dining experiences by building an organization where people are inspired to better their lives." While many organizations have grandiose mission statements, Panda is very purposeful about developing shared leadership. One mechanism it uses involves creating temporary cross-functional teams to tackle important organizational issues as part of its custom executive education program for rising stars. The company has more than quadrupled in size in the past decade and currently has more than 1,800 locations, demonstrating the economic importance of comprehensive shared leadership. Panda focuses on how to infuse shared leadership throughout an entire culture, and the side benefit is high growth. It's a true role model of the corporate American Dream.

Panda represents the paradox of how to balance an economic/strategic perspective with concern for all the stakeholders of the organization. To be sure, all their managers are held accountable for economic results: Same-store sales (SSS), the ubiquitous measure of financial performance in the retail sector, is constantly monitored, and people are rewarded for hitting financial targets. Having said that, if you're not a people person and you're not concerned about your local community, doing outreach to schools and hospitals and the like, you just don't fit the culture. Panda truly illustrates how to integrate responsibility for both profits and people, and that's why employees are so committed to the company's mission of being a place where people are "inspired to better their lives," trusting that financial growth will simply follow.

Seven Steps to Shared Leadership

So what's the best way to go about developing shared leadership? In Figure 17 we detail seven key steps, providing a thorough guide for developing shared leadership in your group or organization.

Step 1: Select for character orientation for shared leadership.

Clearly, selecting the right people is paramount to any endeavor. With shared leadership, however, what constitutes the right people is somewhat different from what you might expect. While it's always sensible to select people with the task, leadership, and followership skills that are required for the work at hand, these skills take a back seat when selecting for shared leadership. That's why we use the term *orientation* in this step, as opposed

Figure 17. These seven steps will help you develop effective shared leadership in your group or organization.

to the terms *knowledge, skills,* and *abilities* (KSAs) that human resources departments use when talking about the "right people." We believe that most people can learn most skills, but their orientation toward tasks and people is based more on their character.

A primary challenge for shared leadership is that it requires the individuals involved to be able to keep their egos in check and work toward a common cause. This, however, is not at all easy to do, particularly when the people involved are bright and very capable. But it's critical that people set aside their egos in order to shift their focus from "Me" to "We."

Step 2: Select for task, leadership, and followership KSAs.

Obviously, if individuals are going to share leadership they must also have the necessary knowledge, skills, and abilities for the tasks at hand. Otherwise you would simply have the proverbial blind leading the blind. That said, besides task-relevant KSAs, the individuals involved in sharing leadership need to possess well-developed listening skills in order to effectively receive leadership from others, which is the cornerstone of shared leadership.

Furthermore, individuals must have a healthy respect for the ideas and perspectives of others. And all of this is for naught if they're hesitant to provide leadership to others. Without the gumption (and self-leadership) to provide leadership it simply doesn't matter how smart a person is – their knowledge will be wasted, and shared leadership will fail. They must be willing to voice their perspective while stepping forward to lead and listen to others while stepping back to follow. In other words, they must be comfortable both leading and following. They must be open-minded. They must not be thin-skinned. They must desire to share the lead.

You might be in the situation of inheriting a group, in which case you won't be able to select the people in the group. But having a clear idea of the orientations and KSAs that promote shared leadership does provide a guide for future selection. Moreover, in the short term, it's possible to nudge people in the direction of the desired orientations and KSAs through targeted training and development efforts, while moving forward on the other steps toward shared leadership.

Step 3: Create shared vision.

If a group is to coalesce around common goals, they need a common vision and purpose as their guides. Research shows us how profoundly a common vision impacts many group dynamics, facilitating positive dynamics and mitigating negative ones. With that said, most organizational leaders overestimate the extent to which vision is truly shared.

While a common vision can start to be formulated by a hierarchical leader, the involvement of group members is extremely important because it enhances ownership, commitment, and persistence. So it's important to engage others in creating the vision – a shared vision – rather than relying on a top-down vision. A shared vision helps to guide action in the face of ambiguous signals from the environment, and it has a clearly documented, positive impact on performance.

Step 4: Focus on core values, especially mutual respect and trust.

Core values contribute to a common perception of what the group stands for, why it exists. They help to buttress the group's resiliency in difficult times, and strengthen its members' resolve to achieve its vision. Core values help to distinguish the group – whether it's a small group, a larger unit, an over-arching organizational entity, or even a society – from other groups. These core values then become a source of long-term competitive advantage, assuming that they are positive values that are difficult for others to copy.

Mutual respect and interpersonal trust are critical values for the development of shared leadership in groups and teams. Emerging research from neuro-economics has even demonstrated that trust is linked to the economic success of nations and societies. Since small groups are the fundamental building blocks of larger so-cial entities, they are where the basics of trust must be built. An important component of trust building is open communication, which helps to generate an ebb and flow of ideas within a group and keeps people from second-guessing others in the knowledge-creation process.

Step 5: Build an awareness of who has which KSAs.

If shared leadership is to function effectively, the people involved need to know to whom they should look for leadership for any particular task or situation, i.e., who has the most-relevant KSAs. Scholars use the term trans-active memory system to indicate the extent to which people are aware of who has the most relevant KSAs for a particular topic. Transactive memory is necessary for leadership to transition to the most appropriate person(s) for a given task.

It's all well and good to say that leadership should be shared, but it's imperative that the correct person be leading at the correct time, based on their knowledge of the task at hand, and not on personality or some other non-pertinent factor. So how do group members en-sure that the correct leader for a given task is identified? By having group norms that encourage the debate of ideas among members of the group. Research clearly demonstrates that having these norms drives creativity and innovation and develops a keen awareness of what each group member has to contribute. Transactive memory, and constantly improving it through active debate, enables groups to proceed to the next step in the development process.

Step 6: Embrace continuous learning.

Shared leadership requires a learning orientation, as opposed to a strict, myopic focus on performance. By embracing learning, a more robust leadership infrastructure is developed, which enables the group to absorb the inevitable shocks to the system, such as the turnover of key personnel. Here we want to emphasize that continuous education, training, and development are important for all employees, not just those in formally designated leadership positions. In a similar vein, the organization needs to engage in evaluation as a tool for development and intervention (360° assessments are one potential mechanism to employ), not as a way to beat up people.

We don't want to give the impression that evaluation should only be used for development. Evaluation plays an important role in judging the contributions of individuals, which might lead to redeployment of some people who don't fit into their current role. Our point is that evaluation is typically not leveraged for learning as much as it can be. Learning is key for the ongoing development, deployment, and delivery of shared leadership.

Step 7: Use group-based rewards to solidify shared leadership.

Compensation is another often-overlooked mechanism for leveraging leadership talent. Here you could utilize group-based compensation, such as gainsharing, that encourages shared leadership within and throughout organizations. Gainsharing is a system that establishes a baseline of productivity and then shares any gains in productivity between the concerned parties, regardless of any outside impact on profits. Productivity is much more under the control of employees than profit and therefore is potentially much more motivating. Gainsharing is just one example.

There are many ways to apply group-based rewards to any group, no matter how big or small. At the micro-level, for example, group celebrations of key milestones can prove an important tool to sustain motivation to keep moving forward. At the larger organization level, profit-sharing and stock ownership can prove useful tools, because they provide stronger identification with the larger organization. The point is that group-based rewards are critical: they help to solidify group identity, group effort, and group success. Research is clear on this. So be creative and identify group-based rewards that complement your particular circumstance.

IN SUMMARY, IT SHOULD BE CLEAR BY NOW that we advocate empowering everyone, at least to some degree. Nearly every single person is capable of taking on some leadership responsibility and contributing to positive organizational outcomes. Encourage those with the most relevant knowledge, not simply those with the highest status, to provide leadership. This means looking beyond artificial borders to tap broad sources of input. Often it means looking outside the organization to involve customers, suppliers, and other important stakeholders in the leadership of the organization. While this can sometimes be uncomfortable, it can also be quite rewarding.

Time to Reflect

Have you ever been part of a group that shared leadership? How did shared leadership develop? What helped to sustain it over time? What was your role in the group? Would you do anything differently after reading this chapter? You might find it helpful to write down some lessons learned so that you can focus on them in your future endeavors.

A PLACE TO RECORD YOUR THOUGHTS

Have you ever been part of a group that shared leadership?

How did shared leadership develop?

What helped to sustain it over time?

What was your role in the group?

Would you do anything differently after reading this chapter?

Chapter 9

ॐ

Socially Responsible
Leadership (S4)

HE FOLLOWING POINTS provide a quick summary regarding the nature of socially responsible leadership:

ॐ Requires being authentic about core values and a higher purpose

ॐ Is based on trust between various stakeholders striving toward common goals

ॐ Entails a long-term perspective that goes beyond short-term performance metrics

ॐ Is built on the concept of respect for others

ॐ Supports the optimum development and utilization of human talent

- ॐ Has regard for the conservation of our planet, as opposed to depletion and disruption
- ॐ Involves serious thought about how to make all systems, processes, and protocols sustainable
- ॐ Causes you to think seriously about the legacy you want to leave

WHY WOULD ANYBODY CARE about socially responsible leadership? Well, if you don't, chaos will ultimately ensue. That's the simple answer. But how about a more pragmatic reason? Most people are inherently attracted to, and motivated by, socially responsible causes. Certain individuals, however, are so self-serving, and so corrupt, that they couldn't care less; after all, they're infected by the leadership disease. Inoculating your group, unit, or organization against the leadership disease requires socially responsible leadership. Perhaps Abraham Lincoln put it best when he said, "You cannot escape the responsibility of tomorrow by escaping it today" (see Figure 18).

So what is socially responsible leadership? It depends on the context, but the basics are simple. Rather than simply focusing on short-term financial returns, socially responsible leaders consider multiple stakeholders'

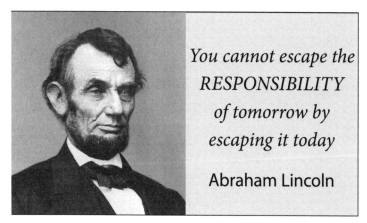

You cannot escape the RESPONSIBILITY *of tomorrow by escaping it today*

Abraham Lincoln

Figure 18. Abraham Lincoln was an early advocate of socially responsible leadership.

interests. Here the research is clear. To the extent that people feel that they're a part of leadership decisions, they're far more willing to both buy into espoused goals and to give plenty of leeway when leaders espouse unconventional goals. The upshot is that people become far more committed to, and psychologically engaged with, socially responsible leadership.

At the same time, there's been a surging interest in the notion of virtues at work. Indeed, there's a growing branch of organizational sciences devoted to the concept of positive organizational scholarship (POS). The folks in this field have found that having a positive orientation to people, planet, and profit has a good influence on people.

So what are the building blocks of socially responsible leadership?

Seven Steps to Socially Responsible Leadership

How do you deploy socially responsible leadership in an organization? Primarily it's an executive-level prerogative, but there's a role for all people, whether inside the organization or as part of the community. The key is to start by building authenticity, transparency, and trust (level-one socially responsible leadership). When these foundational building blocks are in place, the next step is to focus on positive outcomes for people, planet, and profits (level-two socially responsible leadership). Finally, you need to work on making it all sustainable (level-three socially responsible leadership). Figure 19 provides a visual depiction of the seven steps of socially responsible leadership.

Step 1: Establish authenticity.

Without authenticity what do you have? A game, a game of duplicity, cynicism, and double-dealing. By authenticity we don't mean that people should be authentic jerks. To the contrary, we mean that you should find your authentic inner good, and display it. Authenticity requires a bit of soul searching. You need to think very carefully about

Figure 19. These seven steps will help you deploy socially responsible leadership in your organization.

who you are and who you want to be. Then, building on the self-leadership high road, ensure that you act according to how you truly want to be perceived by others.

Step 2: Practice transparency.

Transparency is critical. When actions are opaque people are always guessing about what's taking place behind the curtain. Transparency doesn't mean disclosing every little detail of your life. Rather, in the context of socially responsible leadership, transparency means being clear about the rationales for the decisions you make. It means enabling others around you to see the books, so to speak. It means being honest about mistakes, and enlisting others to help you improve for the future. As a leader you're a role model. Lack of transparency has been closely linked to corruption around the world. The non-profit group Transparency International has been tracking corruption at the nation level. Figure 20 shows their map of the world that documents the perceptions of people regarding the amount of corruption that exists in their countries. The darker the shading in the country, the more corrupt it's believed to be by the people who live there. (There are a couple of exceptions. There is, for example, no data for Greenland or Western Sahara, a disputed territory.)

Leaders should strive to create openness and transparency throughout their interactions with others. The alternative is dismal.

Step 3: Build trust.

Authenticity and transparency greatly facilitate trust. But it takes more than that. You need to prove that you're trustworthy by following through on your commitments,

Science on Socially Responsible Leadership

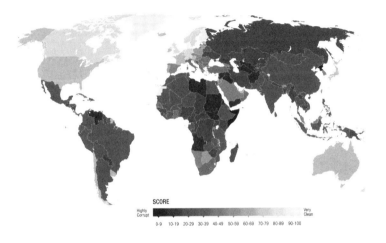

Figure 20. This map shows the perceptions of people regarding the amount of corruption that exists in their countries. Darker areas are more corrupt. Note: The lightest areas on the map (e.g., Greenland and Western Sahara – a disputed territory) are unrated. Source: Transparency International.

or at least by informing people up front when you're not able to do so. Trust is the lubrication for all social interactions. Without trust, the cost of doing business is always higher. People need to hedge, when they don't trust, in order to engage. Neuro-economics research has proven that trust is directly related to economic productivity. Need we say more?

Step 4: Focus on people.

Having established authenticity, transparency, and trust, it's time to focus on the core of socially responsible leadership. The first half of the core involves focusing on people. The key is to do what Peter Drucker advocated decades ago: "Focus on peoples' strengths, and make their weaknesses irrelevant." Everybody has knowledge, skills, and abilities to contribute, and everybody can make a meaningful impact. Force-fitting people into inappropriate roles simply results in frustration and a waste of human talent, which isn't responsible leadership. Unfortunately, not everyone is self-aware enough to have a complete appreciation of their strengths and weaknesses, and they often seemingly set themselves up for failure. As a leader, it's your duty to monitor, coach, and place people in positions where they can thrive.

Step 5: Help protect the planet.

We all have a role in safeguarding our planet. And this role is magnified for leaders. People emulate what they see in leaders. So, as a leader, you must take responsibility for the planet. This doesn't mean that you need to quit your job and start picking up garbage along the freeway. It simply means that you shouldn't purposefully cause environmental damage, and you should be careful with your thinking and decisions about the long term. There are many moral zealots who visibly engage in causes for the environment, only to privately engage in action that's in direct contrast to their public positions. Just be sensible, and help others to do the same.

Step 6: Be profitable.

For an organization to be socially responsible, it must be financially sound and provide the resources necessary for continued operations. If the values, culture, mission, and other intangibles are in place, profits tend to follow . . . but there's certainly no guarantee of this. The organization must offer some concrete value that customers or clients desire. Drucker once said that the three most important questions that must be addressed by any organization are: Who are our customers? What do our customers find of value? And how can we deliver that value? There are no shortcuts. It's an organizational imperative.

Step 7. Ensure sustainability.

While people, planet, and profit are the core of socially responsible leadership, it's all for naught if it's not sustainable. Think carefully about how to establish mechanisms, protocols, and cultural values that will help to sustain your organization's focus on people and planet well beyond any leadership role you occupy. Part of this process harks back to some of the advice we offered earlier regarding the other strands of leadership. For example, you should help to develop leadership in others through utilizing SuperLeadership to encourage self-leadership and shared leadership, thereby engaging them in the leadership process and creating a more robust leadership system that's able to absorb shocks to the system. Your true legacy is to ensure the sustainability of socially responsible leadership. Of course, profits are important to sustainability as well.

Time to Reflect

Socially responsible leadership takes work. In what ways have you demonstrated a strong social responsibility orientation? What were the challenges? How would you advise people who are facing moral dilemmas? What are the keys to ensuring that you maintain a socially responsible stance on leadership? Take some time, right now, to write down advice that will help you engage in socially responsible leadership.

A PLACE TO RECORD YOUR THOUGHTS

In what ways have you demonstrated social responsibility?

What were the challenges?

How would you advise people who are facing moral dilemmas?

How will you maintain a socially responsible stance on leadership?

Part Three

❧

Pulling It All Together

S O FAR we've told you all about the leadership disease, and we've shown you how the over-emphasis on a centralized, top-down model of leadership is fraught with perils. We've also presented the cure – twisted leadership – with its four Ss: self-leadership, SuperLeadership, shared leadership, and socially responsible leadership. These four Ss, however, work best when they're integrated with one another. In fact, similar to our rope metaphor first introduced at the beginning of the book, the Ss are like synergistic strands that, when twisted together, can create a formidable rope. Remove any one of them and strength and sustainability will be greatly reduced. In this section, then, we'll specify how to combine the forces of the four Ss for maximum benefit.

Chapter 10

಄

Integrating the Four Ss of Twisted Leadership

I T WOULD BE FOOLHARDY to suggest that any of the four Ss of twisted leadership could, by themselves, completely inoculate organizations against leadership failure and against the potential for corruption and abuse of power that can stem from centralized leadership. Much like the medications we take for physical illnesses, there are limitations to their effectiveness. But we'll show how, by integrating the four Ss, we can create a highly effective cure for the leadership disease.

In the context of the leadership disease, a major problem we face is that many people who are attracted to leadership roles are those who desire power in order to lord it over others, and they resist attempts to restrain their power. As a personal example, one of the authors engaged in whistle blowing to expose the abuse of power and corruption of a leader to whom he reported – he was fired. Does he have any regret for attempting to administer the correct medicine? Absolutely not. After all, who wants to be associated with corruption? We all need the moral courage to do the right thing. Nonetheless, if we find ourselves in positions where the top leader is immoral and impervious to intervention, it's time to move on.

Below we describe an organization that has deliberately developed and integrated all four Ss of twisted leadership – W. L. Gore and Associates.

Twisted Leadership in Action: W. L. Gore and Associates[5]

W. L. Gore and Associates is a particularly notable case of twisted leadership. Gore is characterized by shared leadership throughout the organization, with a heavy reliance on employee self-leadership within a team-oriented culture. They also have a strong orientation toward socially responsible causes, and SuperLeadership is the norm for people in hierarchical positions.

This highly successful and innovative provider of wide-ranging product offerings, from electronic wire and cable, to industrial and medical products, to fabrics for outdoor sporting activities, relies upon the initiative of all Gore employees (referred to as associates). Elsewhere described as being an "unstructured" company that practices "unmanagement," Gore encourages its workforce to creatively explore possible applications for the primary material used in its products – Gore-Tex – which leads to a continuously growing and evolving array of product offerings. In an article that appeared in *Fast Company,* one newly hired associate described her surprise, especially having come from a traditionally run business, that she had no clear sense of who did what and that she wasn't formally assigned a boss. She kept asking who her boss was until her sponsor (the person who brought her into the company) told her to "stop using the B-word."

Gore may well be the flattest substantial organization in the world. Shared leadership and self-leadership are its central influence principles. A SuperLeadership orientation of assigned leaders allows and encourages organization members to lead themselves to initiate new product ideas by going directly to, and teaming with, whomever they feel can help their project, without having to go through a chain of command. And, as needed at different stages and consistent with shared leadership, these associates step forward to offer leadership based on their expertise and experience, without having to be formally designated as a leader within the firm's structure. All associates are treated as knowledge workers who are capable of helping to create a promising future for the company through the discovery and creation of innovative new products that are in line with the overarching social responsibility values of the company. And they're allowed and encouraged to provide leadership for one another (both shared leadership and SuperLeadership) as the situation and work process require.

Usually leadership is viewed as an outward process involving the influence of formally designated leaders on followers. However, Gore embraces a style that's consistent with the four Ss of twisted leadership, recognizing that all associates have some capacity to lead themselves and each other. This self-influence-based view is reflective of the new requirements of knowledge-based work contexts, and it's a critical part of capturing the optimal potential of leadership influence in contemporary organizations. Going beyond more-common participative and empowerment approaches, Gore has truly created a whole company of leaders.

Even CEO Terri Kelly views herself as primarily an associate, just like everyone else at Gore, even though she's the top executive. Kelly points out that Gore is so diversified that it's not practical or feasible for a CEO to have the knowledge needed to lead in a leader-centric way. According to Kelly, traditional leadership models not only don't fit Gore but they would also impede the innovation process that serves as the lifeblood of the company. She embraces a style consistent with Super-Leadership and socially responsible leadership, facilitating an overall direction for the firm and making sure that the right people are in the right positions to tap the full knowledge of the organization. Empowerment and distribution of authority are key leadership themes for her. And the shared-influence example she sets is highly visible throughout the company.

A distinctive part of the Gore culture is that it embraces the opportunity for any individual to challenge the status quo in the spirit of optimal creativity and innovation. This can lead to lively discussions with much give and take as associates on current product teams, focused on ideas rather than people, respectfully share counter views with each other in order to move the innovation process forward. One associate said that healthy debate is a sign of a good team in the company. Healthy disagreement around current thinking is an important part of the creative process at Gore. For example, after singing the praises of the company's flexible empowering and creative environment, another associate went so far as to say that at times "there is conflict at Gore. People disagree. People (sometimes) don't get along. There are shake ups."

Gore, from its inception, has recognized the need to transcend traditional leadership approaches that vest control and influence with designated leaders who are assigned formal hierarchical authority. In fact, an associate noted that the ability to be selfless and to put the ego aside was at the heart of identifying potential leaders at Gore. Meanwhile, another pointed out that involvement in leadership continuously varied, so that one day you might be a leader 25 percent of the time and a follower the other 75 percent, and then find these roles reversed the very next day. Overall, Gore has fostered less dependence on traditional authority figures, which has helped to fortify the company for successfully meeting the challenges posed in today's highly dynamic, competitive, and complex work environments. The secret is their distinct combination of the four Ss – sharing leadership among highly self-led associates who are encouraged and supported by designated leaders acting as SuperLeaders, all under the umbrella of a socially responsible leadership agenda.

The Importance of Balancing the Four Ss of Twisted Leadership

There are some potentially negative side effects of each of the four Ss of twisted leadership, particularly if not all of the Ss are integrated. We view them as together creating a medical cocktail that requires all the ingredients for a balanced and optimal medication that can cure the leadership disease. If self-leadership, SuperLeadership, shared leadership, and socially responsible leadership are not all well developed, the potential exists for negative side effects such as organizational entropy, self-serving corrupt activities, and unintended groupthink-like social irresponsibility. Our point is that the integration of the four Ss is a balancing act, and you need to constantly monitor the situation, much like a medical doctor monitors the vital signs of a patient.

Accordingly, the four Ss of twisted leadership should interact with and support each other, but they have important limitations when they stand alone. For instance, decision-making dysfunction associated with groupthink in highly cohesive and conforming groups is a real risk if shared leadership is the norm, without the countervailing effects of healthy self-leadership on the part of the members of the group. Displacement of goals can result when groups are low in self-leadership and high on shared leadership. The problem is that group members can overemphasize the need to agree with each other, even in the face of irresponsible decisions. In contrast, the presence of self-leadership can undergird the voicing of contrasting views and the exercising of individual leadership in the group (which reflect personal beliefs, values, and convictions) as opposed to just going along with the general group view, when it's irresponsible. Without the balancing influence of self-leadership, shared leadership can result in unintentional conformity-driven corruption and the abuse of power.

On the other hand, when shared leadership is absent, self-leadership can promote individual members' self-serving behavior. This is especially true when members are driven by personalized (self-serving) power. Indeed, some individuals who are driven by personalized power and skilled at self-leadership may be prone to inappropriate self-serving behavior and unethical acts in the absence of counter-balancing shared leadership. And corruption can come from multiple sources as a consequence. In extreme cases, self-serving, power-driven individuals, when they're spread throughout an organization, could increase nefarious tendencies beyond what might occur under highly centralized leadership. This represents another toxic strain of leadership disease.

Similarly, SuperLeadership, in the absence of socially responsible leadership, can simply result in empowerment gone wild. Empowering people without a clear agenda focused on socially responsible goals and higher-level values can lead to chaotic or dysfunctional outcomes. Indeed, leader empowerment of employees toward value-devoid efforts to increase sales at all costs could result in much more harm than good. For example, imagine unanchored SuperLeadership resulting in employees working to create a dangerous product that could succeed through increasing addiction in under-tapped markets, such as creating new forms of opioids, or new on-label uses of opioids for less severe discomforts, or advocating prescriptions for extended courses of treatment and/or high-strength dosages, all made available through insurance and welfare programs. Prescription opioid use in the United States has more than quintupled since 1980 – just look at the wreckage our society could face from just this one example. People need to coalesce around constructive unifying themes if they're to engage in positive behavior and achieve sustainable, and healthy, synergy and productivity.

Let's look at the flipside, where there's a clear enunciation of a socially responsible cause, but nobody is empowered to do anything. A great cause under a top-down micro-manager will ultimately lose steam. Just one of many reasons this is the case is that socially responsible causes often rely, at least in part, on volunteers. Volunteer (and paid) workers generally want a chance to make choices and express their views or they'll lose interest, stop caring, and eventually go away. Likewise, a great cause in the absence of skilled self-leaders is unlikely to ever gain traction, and without effective teamwork driven by shared leadership, it's likely to achieve only mediocre results.

All four Ss of twisted leadership are essential for a healthy leadership system. Remove any of them and, like our strong, multi-strand rope, the rest are likely to unravel.

Situational Factors and Twisted Leadership

Keep in mind that there are situational factors that affect when twisted leadership is most helpful and appropriate and when it's not. While it can be very helpful for addressing many leadership challenges in contemporary knowledge- and team-based organizations, twisted leadership has its limits. Some of the primary situational factors influencing when it does and doesn't fit well with current demands include the degree of interdependence in the work system, the extent to which creativity is involved, employee commitment, complexity, and urgency. In general, twisted leadership tends to be more effective when interdependence is high, creativity is needed, employees are committed, and there exists significant complexity. It's also better suited for situations where urgency is relatively low. That said, twisted leadership supports further development of capable self-leaders, SuperLeaders, shared leaders, and socially responsible leaders, who proactively solve problems and tap opportunities, resulting in significantly reduced urgency and increased performance and effectiveness in the longer term.

Chapter 11

৯

Prescriptions for Your Own
Twisted Leadership

L EADERSHIP DEVELOPMENT is essential for guarding against corruption and abuse of power. Currently, most leadership development is provided for people who have been identified as candidates for hierarchical leadership roles or who already occupy formal leadership positions. But leadership development needs to be applied across a much wider range of people. Opportunities to learn leadership skills need to be made available to the whole workforce, which represents a very important and too-often-neglected source of leadership in the knowledge age. The time has come to tap the knowledge, experience, and creative potential of everyone so that an organization can better compete and achieve more optimal results. Further, tapping the

Figure 21. The integration of the four strands of leadership is necessary for creating a well-designed, *sustainable* twisted leadership capability.

potential of the wider workforce is the best way to develop the leaders of the future.

Leadership development responsibility also falls in the domain of universities, not just business, government, and not-for-profit organizations. The perspectives, approaches, and skill sets we focus on in our leadership training and development programs are a source of significant input for evolving leaders who help to shape the cultural environments of their organizations. Perhaps the relative lack of attention to constructive approaches to leadership, approaches that extend beyond centralized, top-down models and that better address the current challenges of knowledge-based and team-oriented work that managers so often face, accounts for the widespread dissatisfaction with leaders in organizations. Research results consistently show that leadership is among the most dissatisfying aspect of employees' organizational lives, second only to dissatisfaction with pay. These results apply to a wide range of settings, including employees in professional and technical areas, machine trades, service contexts, and even among managers themselves. Significantly more attention needs to be placed on leadership development. And this is all the more true when organizations strive to go beyond hierarchical, top-down leader approaches, toward emphasis on self-leadership and shared leadership, combined with SuperLeadership and socially responsible leadership. To achieve the full benefits of twisted leadership, effective development of leaders is needed at all levels.

Providing relevant learning opportunities for the leadership strands highlighted in this book is especially important. Self-leadership skills, effective shared leadership philosophy and behaviors, and the core empowering leadership practices of SuperLeadership must be taught. The efficacy of this approach needs to be undergirded by adult-oriented learning methods that reinforce the concepts and skills being taught; these include participative learning methods that involve participants in discussing applications to their real-life problems, self-designed projects where participants identify and apply twisted leadership strategies to personal challenge areas, etc. Also, modeling constructive leadership in learning environments is important. Research has demonstrated that, for better or worse, hierarchical leadership has a causal effect, and followers tend to adopt and even imitate the leadership behavior they experience from above. On the dark side of this equation, we have documented that the best predictor of follower-aversive leadership, such as using intimidation and threats, is the designated leader's use of aversive leadership. Thus, leadership behaviors of persons in positions of authority can spread throughout organizations as others emulate the actions of their leaders. Accordingly, the content of leadership development helps to shape current leadership practices, as well as the leadership of tomorrow, as aspiring leaders rise through their organizations. As a result, these aspiring leaders either feed or help inoculate organizations against the spread of corrupt behavior and the leadership disease. Leaders must recognize that they are role models, whether they like it or not.

We can raise several other important calls to action. For example, from the outset one of our primary intentions was to shine light on the importance of what we called medicine for curing the leadership disease and its manifestations – corruption, abuse of power, and waste of human talent. In particular, we proffered that the four primary ingredients of twisted leadership – self-leadership, SuperLeadership, shared leadership, and socially responsible leadership – each offer significant ameliorating influences on corruptive tendencies, particularly those stemming from centralized, top-down leadership. It's also very important that leadership development directly addresses the curative relationships between each of the four Ss and CSIR (corporate social ir-responsibility).

A focus on the capabilities unleashed by each of the four Ss is also very important. A key aspect of leadership development should be to determine how different organizational contexts and factors influence the proper balance of the four Ss. For example, the degree of emphasis on self-leadership and shared leadership is partly determined by how much task interdependence exists. When interdependence is high, shared leadership may increase in importance relative to self-leadership in order to help distribute power effectively and guard against negative tendencies, as well as to promote higher performance. When the reverse exists, when task interdependence is low, shared leadership may be less important than self-leadership.

And SuperLeadership practices can play a crucial role in leading others toward the right balance of self-leadership and shared leadership, while socially responsible leadership keeps the whole influence process aligned with a solid ethical base. These are important considerations to raise in learning environments, such as training or mentorship programs. Overall, it seems clear that the four Ss of twisted leadership deserve more attention in the development of leaders, and twisted leadership provides a timely guiding perspective to help mitigate potential deleterious tendencies in organizations. Twisted leadership makes clear that it's time to move beyond the moribund myth of heroic, top-down leadership, and the disastrous outcomes it can foster.

OUR TRADITIONAL MODELS OF LEADERSHIP are very simple. There's a person at the top of a hierarchical structure and others are under the leader – they are subordinate – and are expected to follow the direction, goals, and visions of the leader. These leaders, who obtained the role through means such as birth, ownership, position, performance, or political savvy, project influence downward. They must determine how to motivate and guide those below them to achieve organizational goals. But the world has changed, and recent research has revealed a need for a more engaging and inclusive form of leadership in the age of knowledge work. Lines between leaders and followers (who often know more and are in a better position to exercise leadership over themselves and others at key points of work processes) have become blurred. The time for a new kind of twisted leadership has arrived that works with and for everyone.

Where Do We Go From Here?

Collaboration-based approaches and structures in organizations have significantly increased in recent years. This is partly due to more complex and changing environments that call for greater organizational flexibility. However, tapping the optimum potential of the workforce through true empowerment and teamwork poses many challenges and is difficult to achieve. The time has come to question whether current, overly top-down, hierarchically based views of leadership are appropriate any longer. We have proposed an alternate form of leadership better suited for the knowledge age – twisted leadership. The model of twisted leadership is based on integrating four complimentary strands of leadership (the four Ss), which takes us from singular approaches that fit a limited range of situations to an intertwined system of leadership that is strong and sustainable and can be adapted to fit across situations (see Figure 22). Will the implementation of twisted leadership be challenging and at times painful? Unfortunately, for many organizations the answer is yes. The alternative, however, is ultimately more painful.

Does all this mean that hierarchical leadership is an endangered species, that it's about to become extinct? Our answer is unambiguously no. It's not a matter of choosing between hierarchical leadership and twisted leadership – a cornerstone of effective twisted leadership can be the SuperLeadership of hierarchical leaders, who act as champions of the four Ss in their organizations. The issue is, what is currently the most appropriate balance of the four Ss of twisted leadership? By addressing this issue in your own group or organization, you will help to cure the leadership disease and move toward a more appropriate practice of leadership in the age of knowledge work.

We hope that you've found the chapters in this book instructive regarding how twisted leadership can and

Figure 22. Each of the four strands of leadership can be valuable in certain situations, but in the long run you want to move to the reinforced strength and sustainability of intertwined twisted leadership.

should work, and that you've learned how to navigate the primary challenges to its implementation. Together we've begun to take an epic journey. Is it time for your group or organization to begin its own twisted leadership journey, with all the potential payoffs it offers for all involved? Only you can answer that question.

Endnotes

❧

1. Section adapted from Pearce, C. L., and Manz, C. C. 2014. "Introduction to Shared Leadership." In: Pearce, C. L., Manz, C. C., and Sims, Jr., H. P. *Share, Don't Take the Lead.* Charlotte: Information Age Publishing.

2. Manz, C. C. 2015. "Taking the Self-Leadership High Road: Smooth Surface or Potholes Ahead?" *The Academy of Management Perspectives* 29: 132–51.

3. Wrzesniewski, A., and Dutton, J. E. 2001. "Crafting a Job: Revisioning Employees as Active Crafters of Their Work." *Academy of Management Review* 26(2): 179–201.

4. Gagné, M., and Deci, E. 2005. "Self-Determination Theory and Work Motivation." *Journal of Organizational Behavior* 26: 331–62.

5. Case adapted from material appearing in Shipper, F., and Manz, C. C. "W. L. Gore and Associates: A Case Study" (copyright held by authors) and Paulson, R., Wajdi, H., and Manz, C. C. 2009. "Succeeding Through Collaborative Conflict: The Paradoxical Lessons of Shared Leadership." *Journal of Values Based Leadership* 2(1): 59–74.

Resources

༅

Self-Leadership

֍ Manz, C. C. 2015. "Taking the Self-Leadership High Road: Smooth Surface or Potholes Ahead?" *The Academy of Management Perspectives* 29(1): 132–51.

֍ Manz, C. C. 1986. "Self-Leadership: Toward an Expanded Theory of Self-Influence Processes in Organizations." *Academy of Management Review* 11(3): 585–600.

֍ Neck, C. P., Manz, C. C., and Houghton, J. D. 2017. *Self-Leadership: The Definitive Guide to Personal Excellence.* San Francisco: Sage.

֍ Stewart, G. L., Courtright, S. H., and Manz, C. C. 2011. "Self-Leadership: A Multilevel Review." *Journal of Management* 37(1): 185–222.

֍ Manz, C. C., Houghton, J. D., Neck, C. P., Fugate, M., and Pearce, C. L. 2016. "Whistle While You Work: Toward a Model of Emotional Self-Leadership." *Journal of Leadership & Organizational Studies* 23(4): 374–386.

SuperLeadership

- Neck, C. P., Manz, C. C., and Houghton, J. D. 2017. *Self-Leadership: The Definitive Guide to Personal Excellence.* San Francisco: Sage: 193–200.

- Manz, C. C., and Sims, H. P., Jr. 2001. *The New Super-Leadership: Leading Others to Lead Themselves.* San Francisco: Berrett-Koehler.

- Manz, C. C., and Sims, H. P., Jr. 1991. "SuperLeadership: Beyond the Myth of Heroic Leadership." *Organizational Dynamics* 19(4): 18–35.

- Vecchio, R., Justin, J., and Pearce, C. L. 2010. "Empowering Leadership: An Examination of Mediating Mechanisms within a Hierarchical Structure." *Leadership Quarterly* 21(3): 530–42.

Shared Leadership

- Pearce, C. L., Manz, C. C., and Sims, H. P., Jr., 2014. *Share, Don't Take the Lead.* Charlotte: Information Age Publishing.

- Pearce, C. L. 2004. "The Future of Leadership: Combining Vertical and Shared Leadership to Transform Knowledge Work." *Academy of Management Executive* 18 (1): 47–57.

꙰ Pearce, C. L., and Conger, J. A., eds. 2003. *Shared Leadership: Reframing the Hows and Whys of Leadership.* Thousand Oaks, CA: Sage.

꙰ Pearce, C. L., and Wassenaar, C. L. 2014. "Leadership, Like Fine Wine, Is Something Meant to Be Shared, Globally." *Organizational Dynamics* 43(1): 9–16.

Socially Responsible Leadership

꙰ Pearce, C. L., Wassenaar, C. L., and Manz, C. C. 2014. "Is Shared Leadership the Key to Responsible Leadership?" *Academy of Management Perspectives* 28(3): 275–88.

꙰ Pearce, C. L., and Wegge, J. 2015. "Where Do We Go From Here: Is Responsibility Sustainable?" *Organizational Dynamics* 44(2): 156–60.

꙰ Pearce, C. L., and Stahl, G. 2015. "The Leadership Imperative for Sustainability and Corporate Social Responsibility: Challenges Facing the Leaders of Tomorrow." *Organizational Dynamics* 44(2): 83–86.

꙰ Pearce, C.L., and Manz, C.C. 2011. "Leadership Centrality and Corporate Social Ir-Responsibility (CSIR): The Potential Ameliorating Effects of Self and Shared Leadership on CSIR." *Journal of Business Ethics* 102(4): 563–79.

W. L. Gore and Associates

≫ Shipper, F., Stewart, G. L., and Manz, C. C. 2014. "W. L. Gore and Associates Has Created an Entire Shared Leadership Structure." In Pearce, C. L., Manz, C. C., and Sims, H. P., Jr., 2014. *Share, Don't Take the Lead.* Charlotte: Information Age Publishing: 125–45.

≫ Shipper, F., Manz, C. C., and Stewart, G. L. 2014. "Developing Global Teams to Meet 21st Century Challenges at W. L. Gore & Associates." In Shipper, F., et al. 2014. *Shared Entrepreneurship: A Path to Engaged Employee Ownership.* New York: Palgrave Macmillan: 267–84.

Index

෨

Index

About the Authors

❧

Charles C. Manz, Ph.D., is a speaker, consultant, and bestselling author of over 200 articles and scholarly papers and more than 20 books, including *Self-Leadership: The Definitive Guide to Personal Excellence; The New Super-Leadership; Share, Don't Take the Lead; The Power of Failure; Fit to Lead; Business Without Bosses; The Leadership Wisdom of Jesus, Third Edition; Foreword Reviews* magazine best-book-of-the-year Gold Award winner *Emotional Discipline;* and Stybel-Peabody National Book Prize-winner *SuperLeadership.* His work has been featured on radio and television and in the *Wall Street Journal, Fortune, U.S. News & World Report, Success, Psychology Today, Fast Company,* and several other national publications. He is the Nirenberg Chaired Professor of Leadership in the Isenberg School of Management at the University of Massachusetts Amherst. Formerly a Marvin Bower Fellow at the Harvard Business School, his clients have included 3M, Ford, Xerox, General Motors, P&G, American Express, the Mayo Clinic, Banc One, the U.S. and Canadian governments, and many others.

Craig L. Pearce, Ph.D., is a speaker, consultant, and entrepreneur. He has published scores of articles and several books, including *Share, Don't Take the Lead; The Drucker Difference;* and *Shared Leadership: Reframing the Hows and Whys of Leadership.* His work has garnered many awards, including the Penn State Alumni Fellow Award, and has been featured prominently in the popular media, including feature articles in the *Wall Street Journal* and the *Financial Times Agenda.* He is the Ben May Distinguished Professor at the Mitchell College of Business, University of South Alabama. He has lectured at Harvard University, Duke University, University of Amsterdam, Vienna University, Peking University, Instituto de Empresa, and many other leading universities around the world. He was the founding Director of the Deloitte Leadership Institute in Istanbul and has consulted for some of the leading organizations of the world, including American Express, the Central Intelligence Agency, Land Rover, Mack Trucks, Panda Express, and many others. He is both a leadership development expert and a leader, drawing from real-life leadership experience building entrepreneurial firms, to inform both his scholarship and his leadership and organizational development practice.